Moon Method Diary 2026

Created by Anna Maria Whitehead

© COPYRIGHT ANNA MARIA WHITEHEAD 2026

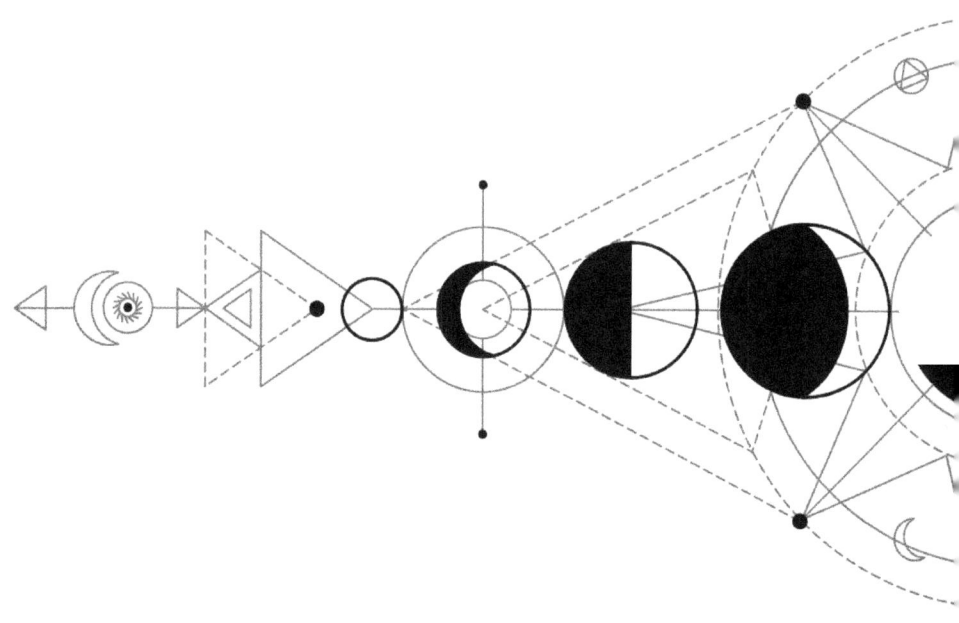

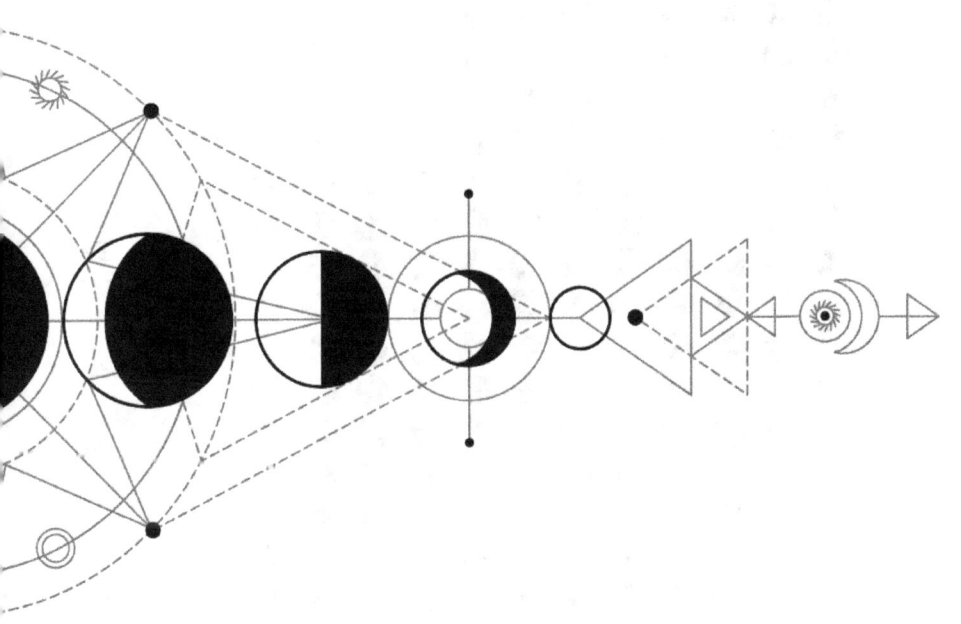

Great Mystery,
Teach me how to trust
my heart,
my mind,
my intuition,
my inner knowing,
the senses of my body,
the blessings of my spirit.
Teach me to trust these things
so that I may enter my Sacred Space
and love beyond my fear,
and thus Walk in Balance
with the passing of each glorious Sun

— Lakota Prayer.

How to Use Your Diary

We live in an age of infinite choice. At dawn inspiration calls us to write, move, meditate, nourish, create new ways to prosper, nurture our loved ones, and weave ourselves into our communities. Technology promised ease, in some ways it has delivered, but it has also opened countless doors encouraging us to do more and be more.

For those who thrive on possibility, the visionaries, the multi-passionate ADHD minds and Manifesting Generators it is easy to say yes too often and our days can overflow into chaos.

The Moon Method Diary was created to be your guide so you can honour your true priorities, aligning your time with your energy, by living in harmony with your own inner cycles, and the cycles, rythms and seasons of Mother Earth.

This diary is not simply a planner it is a ritual, a mirror, and a guide that invites you to get to know and move within your own rhythm. Encouraging you to choose with intention, and to create a life that feels spacious and luminous.

Mantra for Your Practice
*I honour the rhythm of my days.
I choose what matters most.
I move with the moon,
and my life unfolds in harmony.*

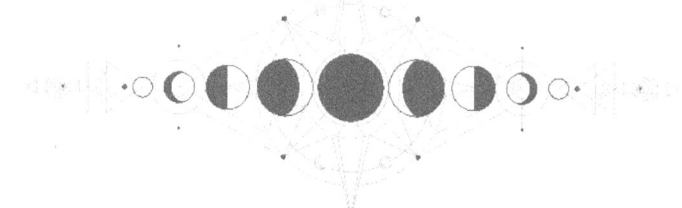

The Monthly Spread is your full moon view - A luminous map of what matters most in the month ahead, allowing you to see clearly where to place your light.

The Weekly Spread is your waxing moon - Refine your intentions and plans, let momentum for the week ahead build and ensure that each job, activity, errand, exercise or ritual receives its devoted moment in your Diary.

The Daily Spread is your new moon - An intimate space where you plant each seed of your day, hour by hour, mindful of the time and care each commitment needs, ensuring that what you promise yourself is possible in the time you have.

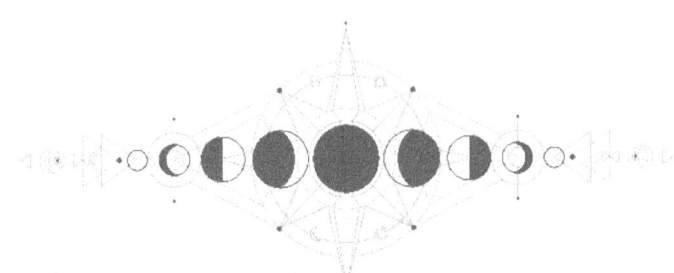

Phases of the moon

New Moon
New beginnings and intention setting. Listen to your intuition.

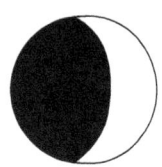
Waxing Moon
Put plans into action.

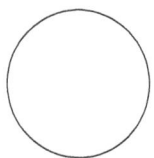
Full Moon
Gratitude for all you have received. Tune in to your heart to discover what you need to release during the waning moon.

Waning Moon
Release anything that no longer serves you.

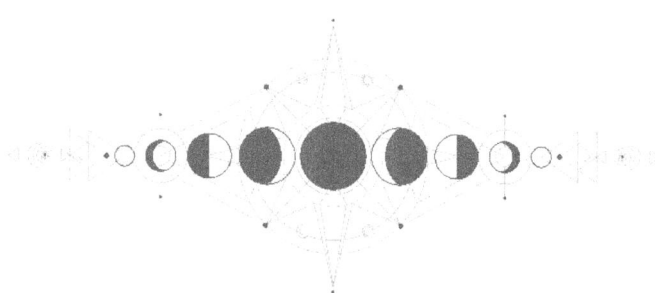

Working with the moon

Live in Sync with Nature to Manifest Your Best Life

Do you ever feel weighed down by endless to-do lists? Have you made plans to see a friend, only to find that when the day arrives your heart longs for stillness instead?

The secret lies in knowing when your energy will be high and when your body will call you to rest, and plan your life accordingly. Just as the moon moves through her phases, we too move through our own cycles. When we learn to listen, nature shows us exactly when to act, create, rest, and reflect.

Our modern world often tells us we should be at our peak every single day, wearing busyness as a badge of honour. But we are not meant to run at one hundred percent all the time. We are cyclical beings, our energy ebbs and flows. Time alone and moments of rest are not indulgences; they are vital, and deserve space in your diary with the same reverence as an important meeting.

When we rest, we replenish. When we align our actions with the rhythms of the moon and our own cycles, we become more productive, more creative, and more at peace. The New Moon is our invitation to pause and plant intentions for the month ahead. From there, we can move forward with renewed clarity, focus, and energy, knowing exactly where we want to go and how to get there.

The aim of this diary is to help you navigate the fullness of life without tipping into burnout, to create a schedule that supports your natural cycles, and to bring you back into flow. When life flows, creativity blooms, joy grows, and abundance comes naturally.

Wishing you a year of harmony, inspiration, and magic.

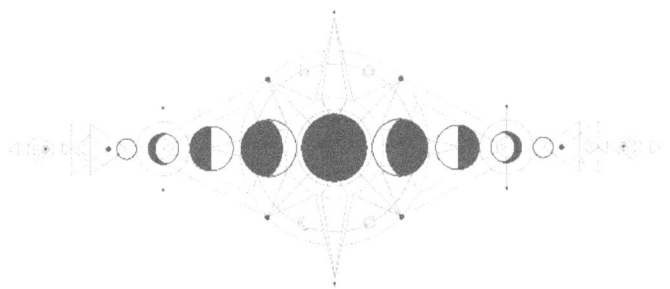

A **New Moon** is a monthly rebirth, a time for new beginnings, ideas and creativity. An opportunity to set your intentions. This is a perfect time to spend alone journaling your thoughts and practicing self care which will mean different things to all of you. Perhaps a morning meditation or an evening bubble bath is all it takes, but whatever it is, make sure to take some time for yourself. In the silence you will receive the intuitive guidance you need. Take some time to set your intentions for the month ahead.

Clear Quartz, a cleansing crystal perfect for clearing the mind and aiding in meditation.

The **Waxing Moon** asks you to act upon the ideas you received during the new moon. This is a perfect time for socialising and communication, so scheduling in meetings would be good during a waxing moon, but be careful not to burnout, eat well during this moon and avoid anything not so good for you.

Citrine, a wonderful crystal for manifesting abundance.

A **Full Moon** is a good time to check in with the intentions you set under the new moon. Consider what finishing touches you need to get you to your goals. Work with your intuition and gut feelings. Get clear on what you need to release when the moon begins to wane. Energies are very high under this powerful full moon phase, so you will have energy for meeting with friends, but you may prefer to use this energy to be at home burning your favourite incense, playing some music, and tuning into your highest self. Full moons are a great time to cleanse the body and mind.

Moonstone, helps to connect to your inner goddess and true meaning.

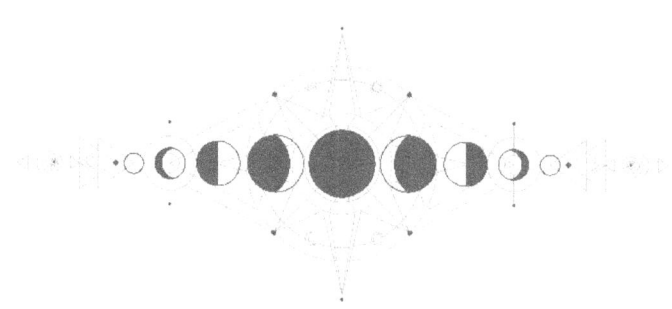

The **Waning Moon** calls you to release that which does not serve you. Pay attention to anything that has stood in the way of your goals and dreams. This is a perfect time to organise, throw things away, consider if you have any toxic elements in your life. Do you need to get rid of any particular bad habits? Now would be the time to start looking at that. Let go of unwanted energy and release.

Rhodonite, a healer related to the heart chakra which helps with forgiveness and releases self-destructive tendencies to help with healing at a soul level.

How amazing is the moon! She provides us with the chance to start afresh every month. We can use her energy to guide us. These points refer to how the moon affects us collectively, but each moon will affect us all differently depending on our own birth charts. You may wish to dive deeper into this with an astrologer as it can be helpful for introspection and making sense of our experiences as we move throughout the year. There is a wonderful group called Lunar Living with bi-weekly moon circles, meditations and much more. See www.lunarliving.com and use my discount code for 11% off - CODE - **ANNA5422**
Valid on the 3 month - 12 month packages.

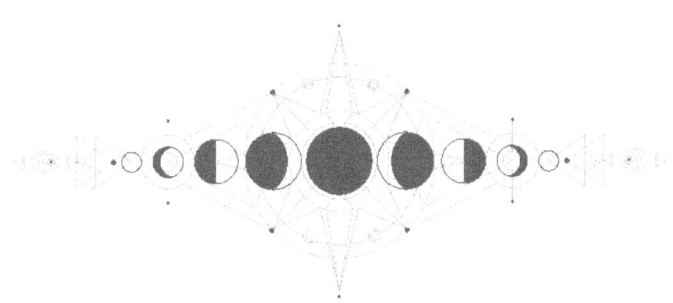

The Moon & The Zodiac

Book recommendations to get you started with astrology - Lunar Living by Kirsty Gallagher, DK Books Astrology by Carol Taylor and for more seasoned astrologers check out the Library of Esoterica, Astrology by Jessica Hundley.

Aries - Birth and Manifestation
Fire Sign

Since Aries sits at the start of the astrological new year this **New Moon** is the perfect time to start anew. A powerful portal for manifesting. Write down those intentions and go after whatever it is you feel passionate about.

An Aries **Full Moon** has a way of bringing our fears and emotions to the surface. The ruling planet of Aries is Mars, there can be warrior energy and a competitive drive that surfaces. You may feel a call to action, but remember to release anything that no longer serves you.

Taurus - Grounded and Earthy
Earth Sign

Being an earth sign the Taurus **New Moon** helps us to feel grounded, and inspires us to cancel out the noise of other opinions so that we can hear what our own inner truth is. Taurus is ruled by Venus, she gives you permission to take care of yourself. If you need it go ahead and take time for yourself. Make sure your needs are being met.

The Taurus **Full Moon** has a habit of bringing insecurities to the forefront, feelings around imposter syndrome and self worth may come up. It can be helpful to sit with these feelings, because we first need to acknowledge them in order to release them.

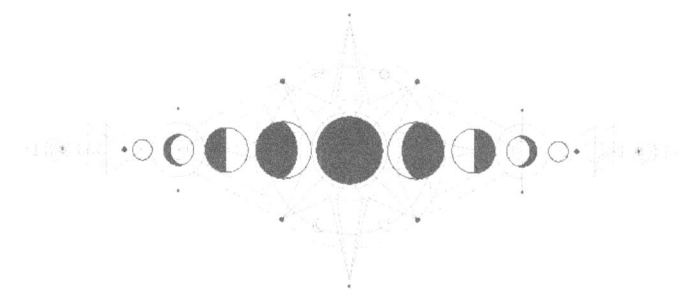

Gemini - Duality, Inspiration and Change
Air Sign

A Gemini **New Moon** can often bring a feeling of excitement and inspiration. If however you are feeling drained and exhausted in the days leading up to this moon, it could be that you want to change something in your life but have been avoiding it. This moon will be eager to get your attention to encourage you to start taking action.

The Gemini **Full Moon** can bring up a lot around communication and knowledge. Pay attention to what thoughts are coming up during this time. Lots of insights can come through, but thoughts may be in overdrive which can feel overwhelming and anxiety inducing. This is a good time to bring limiting beliefs to the surface, but remember to take time out and slow down, perhaps with yoga or breath work to stay centred.

Cancer - Sacred Depths of Intuition and Emotion
Water Sign

The Cancer **New Moon** is very at home in her ruling planet of Cancer. This moon can bring up big emotions, a heightened sense of intuition and feminine power. Self care is important. Spend time alone or with people you can be vulnerable with. Wear your heart on your sleeve and really feel into everything that is stirring within you.

The Cancer **Full Moon** may show you the road ahead. There can be a deep intensity that comes with this full moon. Cancer's intuitive energy helps to light the way. The sun is in Capricorn which brings ambition and visions for the future. Make the most of this combination to make plans for the year, create vision boards, get together with friends and plan summer adventures. Focus on anything that you need to change to get to where you want to be by this time next year.

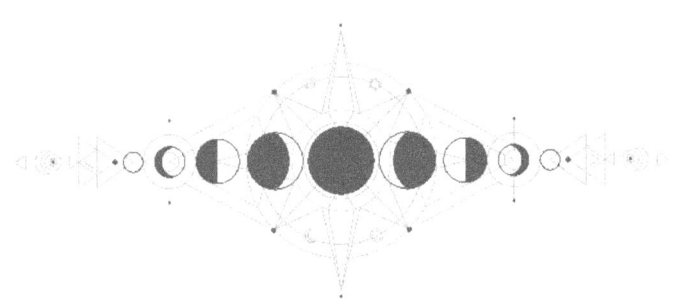

Leo - Charisma, Power and Heart-Centered Energy
Fire Sign

A **New Moon** in Leo brings with it much power. The sun rules Leo, there is so much light, magnetism and energy. If you have been pondering over starting a new job, or adventure then this is the energy to use to get you there.

The **Full Moon** in Leo has fiery energy which asks you to look at your desires beyond the to-do lists. What do you really want out of life? Where have you held yourself back to please others, where have you not lived your biggest dreams? Leo rules the heart and has a tendency to bring your desires to the surface. Spend some time in heart chakra meditation, really listen to what your heart is telling you. There's an element of bravery that comes with a Leo moon that will help you to put yourself first.

Virgo - Perfectionism and Attention to Detail
Earth Sign

Virgo is the healer so a **New Moon** in Virgo offers deep healing for those willing to seek it. Yes, she is critical and we can expect to hear voices of self sabotage. Maybe we tell ourselves that our to do list is too big, we don't have time to sit and reflect during this moon, but if we give ourselves space and get honest, we can see big results. The ruling planet is Mercury which symbolises communication, travel and trade. Whilst Virgo energy brings organisation and focus. Use this combination, get a notepad, make some lists, do a clean out, cleanse your space and make room for your dreams.

The earthy energy of a **Full Moon** in Virgo is so grounded that there is no where to hide from ourselves. This moon is a great time to check in with our lives in general, are we where we want to be? If not then we can use her creative, organisational energy to make a plan. What steps do you need to take to up-level your situation? Watch out for perfectionism and trying to control every outcome.

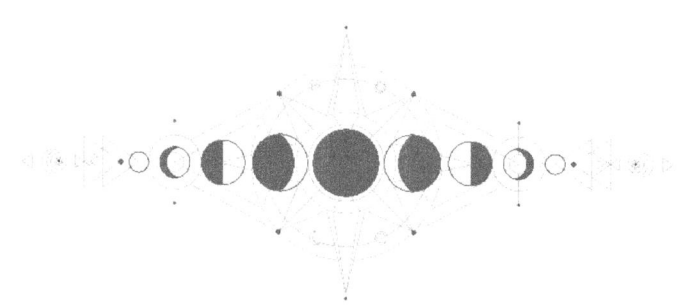

Libra - Balance and Relationships
Air Sign

The **New Moon** in Libra brings up a lot around relationships, boundaries and balance. Use this moon to deepen the relationship you have with yourself. New moons are always a time for self reflection and inner work, but particularly around this Libra moon. Allow your intentions for the rest of the year and beyond to come through and watch out for any triggers that surface, especially around relationships or not speaking your truth.

Since the **Full Moon** in Libra brings with it the energy of balance, it can be good practice to make a note of everything in your life that is important to you, make a circle and create 8 or 10 sections. Such as family life, romantic life, work life, health, fitness, travel, spiritual life etc. Then give a mark from one to ten. When you have finished you will have a picture of your life. It is likely that some areas score highly and others not so much. Where are you thriving? Which areas of your life/relationships do you need to work on?

Scorpio - Death and Rebirth
Water Sign

The **New Moon** in Scorpio is an intense but brilliant moon that calls us to do the deepest shadow work. This often feels daunting. There is no where to run and hide under this moon. Emotions, deeply buried hurts and betrayals from our past can come up. Many people say they fear this moon and how it makes them feel, but really, there is much healing and change on the other side. Pluto the planet of death and destruction rules Scorpio, we can use this energy to make way for the new.

Under this **Full Moon** in Scorpio spend some time in a sanctuary of your choice. Where do you feel safe? Perhaps in your favourite room at home with some incense burning whilst you relax under a duvet listening to music. Perhaps under your favourite tree. Where ever it is, try and carve out some time to yourself in a safe space. Once you are there close your eyes, take some breaths and think about what you need to release from your life. Perhaps it is clutter, a toxic relationship or working too many hours. What do you need to be free from, and how can you gently release yourself from it, so that you can be re-born, free from whatever was weighing you down.

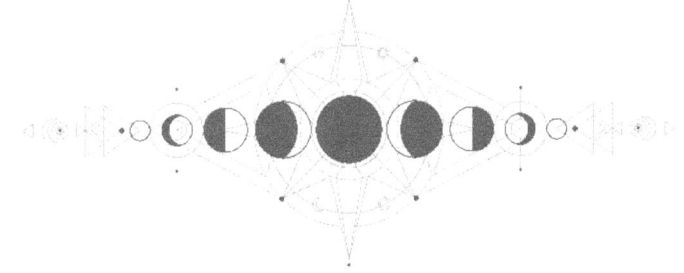

Sagittarius - Adventure and Freedom
Fire Sign

The **New Moon** in Sagittarius brings freedom and adventure, but will highlight anywhere where you feel out of control. Are there systems of authority where you feel you lack autonomy? If so you could feel a bit suffocated by that under this moon. For the travellers and adventure seekers, this is the moon for you. We will be encouraged to get moving, take that trip, do all the big things we've been holding back from.

A **Full Moon** in Sagittarius highlights anywhere where we might feel that we're being controlled, but the sun is in Gemini which brings the energy of change and truth, the ruling planet is Jupiter which symbolises abundance, fortune and expansion. You may feel clarity over a particular action you need to take. Spend some time alone, close out the noise and work out what you need to release, whilst getting clear on what you want to invite in.

Capricorn - Discipline and Self-Sufficiency
Earth Sign

The **New Moon** in Capricorn is a very practical moon which doesn't really like anything too emotional. Get real under this energy about your life purpose and goals. Capricorn is ruled by Saturn which symbolises discipline and limitations. Set your inner practical self free to make plans for the year ahead, you may feel an element of productivity to finally get a certain project off the ground.

Under the **Full Moon** in Capricorn you may feel a need to organise the spaces around you: your home, office, wardrobe. Removing anything that is in your way.
Capricorn is practical and grounded, but the sun is in Cancer which can bring up emotions. If You suddenly start doubting your ability to start your own business or take that solo trip around the world, these doubts could be highlighting fears that have been hidden. Allow yourself to feel anything that comes up and try and find the root cause for these limiting beliefs. EFT is a great technique for dealing with limiting beliefs.

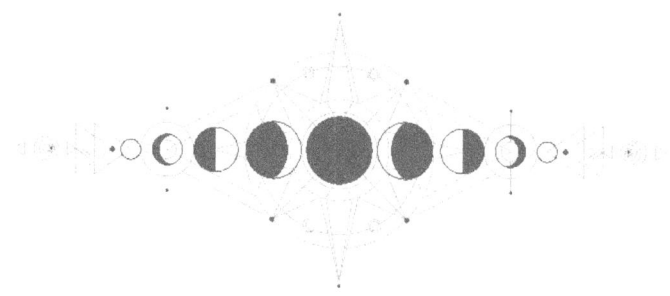

Aquarius - Innovation and Self Expression
Air Sign

The **New Moon** in Aquarius opens the mind to visionary insights and glimpses of what's to come. There's a fiercely independent energy that comes with this moon, so you may find yourself longing for freedom in any areas where that may be threatened. A tendency to rebel often emerges if this is the case.
This moon is a good time to think about your passions, what would you love to spend every day doing? If that's not already your life, what steps can you take to get there?

The **Full Moon** in Aquarius is a moon that brings with it the potential for change. The freedom loving energy of Aquarius shines a light on transformation and possibility, and paired with the Sun in radiant Leo, creates a powerful blend of heart and vision. Listen deeply to your inner truth, and let Aquarius' innovation guide you toward making your heartfelt dreams a reality.

Pisces - Mystical and Dreamy
Water Sign

The **New Moon** in Pisces brings mystical, dreamy energy. The last sign of the zodiac helps you to see into the beyond. The Pisces symbol is two fish swimming in opposite directions, a nod to the hermetic principle 'as above so below'.
Daydream to your hearts content under this whimsical moon, journal about the visions that come through to you. Create vision boards, fill out the manifestation pages in this diary or any other manifestation techniques you like to use. This is a great moon for it.

The Pisces **Full Moon** opens the heart and softens the edges of everyday life. An intuitive moon that invites you to surrender, dream, and trust in what you can't yet see.
It's a time for release and renewal, for letting go of old stories or worries that keep you anchored in the past. Pisces energy encourages forgiveness and a return to compassion.
Rest, dream, create, and let your imagination flow freely. Music, journaling, or being near water can help you process emotions and reconnect with your inner world.

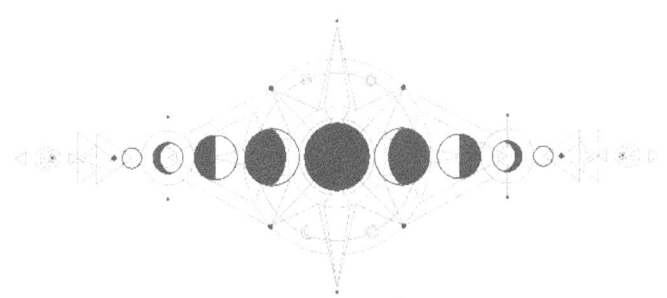

The Blood Mysteries and the Moon

'Your Moon Time'

Follicular - Inner Spring - Maiden - Waxing Moon

Ovulation - Inner Summer - Mother - Full Moon

Luteal - Inner Autumn - Sorceress - Waning Moon

Menstruation - Inner Winter - Crone - New Moon

The White Moon Cycle
Bleed with the new moon - Ovulate with the full moon
Mirroring the moons cycle
Embodying creation whether that be children or ideas and projects that are being brought to life.

The Red Moon Cycle
Bleed with the full moon - Ovulate with the new moon
Embodying the medicine woman. In ancient times this cycle was for the priestess and healers who channelled their energy outwards.

The Pink Moon Cycle
Bleed with the waxing crescent - Ovulate with the waning crescent.
Embodying expansion and spiritual ascension, becoming a new version of yourself.

The Purple Moon Cycle
Bleed with the waning crescent - Ovulate with the waxing crescent
Embodying release and desire for inner reflection.

It is said that during ancient times when we lived in hunter gatherer communities we would all have been in sync experiencing a white moon cycle together, with the exception of the priestess who would have been on the red moon cycle.

Back when there was no light pollution we lived in tune with our circadian rhythms, the outer seasonal cycles and our own inner hormonal cycles. We lived as cyclical beings and women gathered in circle together during their moon time, holding space for each other and shedding all that no longer served them. They would sit in ceremony, their cycle was a spiritual practice.

Today it is recognised that our periods are our fifth vital sign. We know they can tell us a great deal about our health in general. Our energy waxes and wanes through-out the month just like the moon does.

It is good practice to chart our cycles, and this includes those of us who don't have a menstrual cycle. It can still be very beneficial to chart our states of being on a daily basis allowing us to notice any patterns over the period of a few months. This is a useful tool in getting to know subtleties about yourself. You can then use this information to work in harmony with your inner ebbs and flows. For example if you see that you are always exhausted on day twenty, but full of life on day twelve then you can use this information to your advantage.

There is space in this diary to make notes each day. Start on day one of your cycle and write a note on each day about anything you feel you would like to chart, particularly your emotions and energy levels. Try it out and see if you notice a pattern. If you do not have a cycle, perhaps use the new moon as your day one.

Honouring the seasons

Paying close attention to the seasons and creating rituals around them helps us in turn to honour ourselves. We are nature. We are cyclical beings. When we move with the natural rhythms of our Earth, we learn to live in a flow state, in the present. As each season moves into the next on the wheel of the year, we can celebrate these changes outside and inside of ourselves. Equinoxes and solstices allow us to feel at one with the seasons and remind us to check in with ourselves, so rather than mindlessly racing through the year wondering how another one flew by so quickly, working with the seasons can add focus and clarity to these 365 days.

Spring Equinox 20th March

A time when light and dark come into balance and nature blooms with life. Use this time to think about what seeds you want to sow in your own life. How do you want to use this new vital energy to manifest abundance? Spring shows us how to be patient whilst we wait for the little buds to blossom. Emulate nature in this way and be easy on yourself if you are waiting for your manifestations to come to fruition. Try and spend at least ten minutes every day with your bare feet touching the Earth. Take as much time in nature as you can, pausing to pay attention to spring as she emerges from the dark winter. Close your eyes and take in the sounds of nature all around you. Spend time journaling on your goals for the remainder of the year. Are there steps you can now take as you leave winter behind you to get ready to step into the light of spring?

Ritual ideas: Cleanse your space with frankincense or incense of your choice, do a grounding meditation such as a root chakra meditation by imagining that your feet root firmly into the Earth, you could sit with your back against a tree for twenty minutes connecting with the Earth's energy, followed by a cleansing bath with Epsom salts and rose petals.

Summer Solstice 21st June

In the northern hemisphere the Earth's axis is tilted at its closest point from the sun. This is the longest day, and shortest night. Nature is in full bloom all around us and inspires us to put our creative ideas into practice and bring projects to life. Use the heightened energy of the solstice to create and be inspired.

Ritual Ideas: Get outside, walk barefoot through a forest, hold a fire circle with friends. Celebrate nature and each other. Eat fresh food from the Earth and give thanks for all that she provides us. Write lists of everything you are grateful for. What is showing up in abundance for you? Stop and pause to give thanks for it. Get up at sunrise to honour the sun. Perhaps incorporate a yoga session or whatever suits you to move your body. Get creative with your celebrations and make them your own.

Autumn Equinox 23rd September
The first day of autumn is a time for releasing. Get clear on what no longer serves you, and just like the trees who shed their leaves, allow yourself to let go. The days will begin to get shorter and nature invites you to retreat inwards to rejuvenate. There is a different level of energy that we are now heading into, and one of the best ways to honour that time is to reflect on the year so far, and ask what you need to shed to move forward.

Ritual ideas: Write a list of anything you don't want to take with you as we move into this next part of the year, make a bonfire and burn the list. Take a long walk and notice the changes in nature all around you and take home some moss and wood to make an altar for the Earth goddess Gaia. As the nights get shorter and the air gets colder embrace the change in energy and the subtle whispers calling you inwards.

Winter Solstice 21st December
Celebrate the cyclical nature of our world on the longest night before the sun is renewed once more. The winter solstice welcomes a slower pace, honour that. Reclaim the stillness. The darkness of winter can be difficult, try and notice the beauty of the sparse trees and frosty mornings. Treat yourself to comforting foods and special time with loved ones playing board games and embrace the slower, quieter, darker days.

Ritual ideas: Spend some time in silence reflecting on the year so far and your dreams for the year ahead. Head to a beauty spot that you have a connection with and reflect on any changes to this area during winter. Wrap up warm and enjoy a fire, the flames can be very meditative and healing. Shamans say that fire allows for rapid transformation. Make the most of the darkness and any revelations it has helped bring to light.

Wheel of the Year

* Yule - December 21st
Yule is the winter festival celebrating the winter solstice and the returning of the light.

* Imbolc - February 1st - Sunset on February 2nd
This festival marks the beginning of spring. Goddess Bridgid is celebrated with feasts and fires. Green candles are lit in her honour.

* Ostara - March 20th
A solar holiday where we welcome the returning warmth of spring. Goddess Eostre is honoured with alters of flowers, eggs and seeds.

* Beltane - May 1st
The half way mark between the spring equinox and summer solstice. We give thanks to the fertility of the land.

* Litha - June 21st
The longest day of the year. Vikings would pray to Freyja for an abundant harvest and ceremonial plants are used around midsummer bonfires.

* Lammas - August 1st
Represents the midway point between summer and autumn. The time of the first harvest.

* Mabon - September 23rd
The second harvest which lands on the autumn equinox.

* Samhian - October 31st
Better known as halloween this is the Celtic new year and the final harvest. The veil between worlds is at its thinnest, we honour our ancestors on this night.

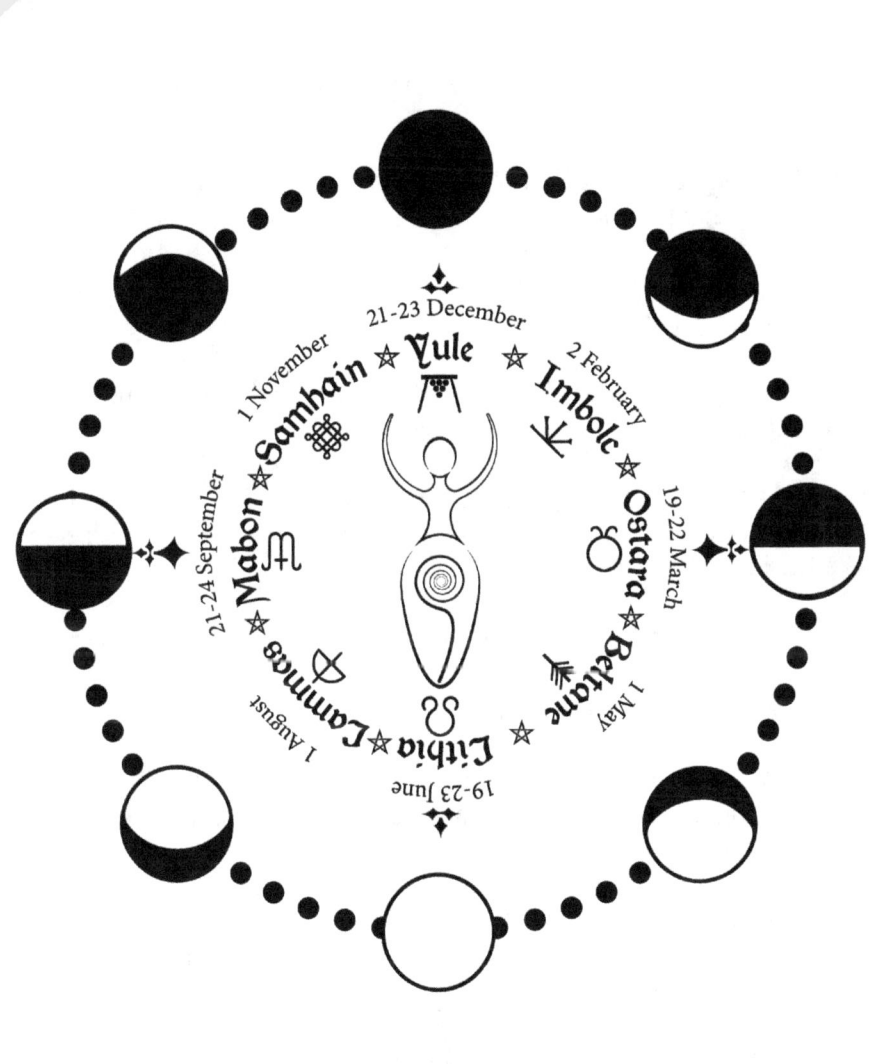

Three ways to manifest your dreams

New Years resolutions are a cultural norm for many of us, but often we find it difficult to commit. It may be that the depth of winter just isn't the right time for making big decisions for the next twelve months. Some of us prefer to write down our visions for the year around the spring equinox when the world around us is coming to life.

There is no right or wrong. Fill in the goals pages at whatever time of year feels right to you.

There are many ways to bring our creative visions to life, and you will find more than one way to manifest your dreams in this diary. Yearly goal setting, seasonal visions plus a vision board.

On the opposite page you can write out your main yearly goal, with space to break it down. Work out what you need to do daily, weekly and monthly to get you to where you want to be by 2027.

There is also space for seasonal inspiration. Spend some time each equinox and solstice quietly observing and making space for inspiration to come through. Take some time out with a warm drink, a candle and something that represents the season, perhaps a flower, certain colours or a crystal, and allow yourself to visualise your desires for the season ahead. As mother Earth moves through her cycles we often find that ideas come to us that we never would have thought of during the darker days around New Year. Manifesting alongside the seasons adds a beautiful dimension to making our dreams a reality.

My main yearly goal is: _____

To achieve this goal by 2027, I will create the following habits to get myself there.

- Daily

- Weekly

- Monthly

Seasonal Vision for 2026

Use this space to write any ideas that come to you throughout the year. From Inspirational business ideas, passion projects or perhaps countries you want to visit.

Winter

Spring

Summer

Autumn

Vision board

Use this space to paint, doodle or cut pictures out of magazines. Whatever works for you. The goal is to create a powerful visualisation tool to aid in manifesting your dreams. You can look at this every day to bring your 2026 goals to life.

Share your vision with us on Instagram @the_moonmethod

"She remembered who she was and the game changed."

— Lalah Delia.

Practices to help you remember what your soul came here to do.

Meditation & Stillness
Creates the space to hear your inner voice. Try sitting quietly, close your eyes, and focus on your breath. Visualise a golden light within your heart, growing with each inhale. As thoughts come and go, allow them to drift without attachment.
If sitting in silence feels hard, try guided meditations or yoga nidra which can help you sink deeper.

Journaling for Self-Inquiry
Journaling bypasses the busy mind and connects you with your inner knowing. Write freely without censoring yourself.
Use prompts like: "Who am I beneath my roles, titles, and responsibilities?" Try writing with your non dominant and see what answers come through to the questions you have.

Spending Time in Nature
Your soul is deeply connected to the earth's cycles. Walk barefoot on the grass, sit under a tree, watch the moon. Listen - not just with your ears, but with your whole being. Nature slows the nervous system and helps you reconnect to the present moment, where your soul resides.

Breathwork & Embodiment
Releases stored energy which can sometimes keep us from hearing our soul. Breathwork, somatic movement, or even gentle dance can help you shift blocked emotions and reconnect to your innate life force. When your body softens and opens, your inner guidance becomes clearer.

January 2026

Notes	Monday	Tuesday	Wednesday
	5	6	7
	12	13	14
	19	20	21
	26	27	28

Thursday	Friday	Saturday	Sunday
1	2	3 ○	4
8	9	10 ☾	11
15	16	17	18 ●
22	23	24	25
29	30	31	1

January
White Buffalo Calf Woman

White Buffalo Calf Woman

Stepping from the horizon with a robe the colour of first snow a man reached for her with hunger and fell into dust. Another bowed to her with an open heart, and she spoke to him in the language of rivers and wind. She carried a Sacred Pipe which acted as a bridge between the hearts of the people and the Sky-Father. She taught the Seven Ways of Balance, prayer, vision, renewal, sacrifice, and love that binds all beings.

When her work was done she turned toward the setting sun and with each step her form shifted: black buffalo, red buffalo, yellow buffalo, and finally white calf.

She promised to return when the world cries for healing. Today when a white buffalo is born, the women feel her stir in their dreams. She is the keeper of sacred ways, the whisper that reminds us that the Divine Feminine waits, patient as the turning of the stars.

Crystal: White Buffalo Turquoise Resonates directly with her imagery and teachings - purity, spiritual wisdom, and connection to the Great Spirit.

My Vision for January

Thursday | 1 January 2026 - Waxing Gibbous

6:00	Today's quick wins
7:00	
8:00	
9:00	
10:00	
11:00	Health and nutrition
12:00	
13:00	
14:00	Today, I am grateful for...
15:00	
16:00	
17:00	Today's self care
18:00	
19:00	
20:00	Chart your cycle
21:00	
22:00	
23:00	Positive affirmation
Notes	

Friday | 2 January 2026 - Waxing Gibbous

6:00	**Today's quick wins**
7:00	
8:00	
9:00	
10:00	
11:00	**Health and nutrition**
12:00	
13:00	
14:00	**Today, I am grateful for...**
15:00	
16:00	
17:00	**Today's self care**
18:00	
19:00	
20:00	**Chart your cycle**
21:00	
22:00	
23:00	**Positive affirmation**
Notes	

Saturday | 3 January 2026 - Full Moon in Cancer at 10.02 GMT

6:00	**Today's quick wins**
7:00	
8:00	
9:00	
10:00	
11:00	**Health and nutrition**
12:00	
13:00	
14:00	**Today, I am grateful for...**
15:00	
16:00	
17:00	**Today's self care**
18:00	
19:00	
20:00	**Chart your cycle**
21:00	
22:00	
23:00	**Positive affirmation**
Notes	

Sunday | 4 January 2026 - Waning Gibbous

6:00	**Today's quick wins**
7:00	
8:00	
9:00	
10:00	
11:00	**Health and nutrition**
12:00	
13:00	
14:00	**Today, I am grateful for...**
15:00	
16:00	
17:00	**Today's self care**
18:00	
19:00	
20:00	**Chart your cycle**
21:00	
22:00	
23:00	**Positive affirmation**
Notes	

My Week 5th Jan - 14th Jan

Mon	
Tue	
Wed	
Thu	
Fri	
Sat	
Sun	

Monday | 5 January 2026 - Waning Gibbous

6:00	**Today's quick wins**
7:00	
8:00	
9:00	
10:00	
11:00	**Health and nutrition**
12:00	
13:00	
14:00	**Today, I am grateful for...**
15:00	
16:00	
17:00	**Today's self care**
18:00	
19:00	
20:00	**Chart your cycle**
21:00	
22:00	
23:00	**Positive affirmation**
Notes	

Tuesday | 6 January 2026 - Waning Gibbous

6:00	Today's quick wins	
7:00		
8:00		
9:00		
10:00		
11:00	Health and nutrition	
12:00		
13:00		
14:00	Today, I am grateful for...	
15:00		
16:00		
17:00	Today's self care	
18:00		
19:00		
20:00	Chart your cycle	
21:00		
22:00		
23:00	Positive affirmation	
Notes		

Wednesday | 7 January 2026 - Waning Gibbous

6:00	**Today's quick wins**
7:00	
8:00	
9:00	
10:00	
11:00	**Health and nutrition**
12:00	
13:00	
14:00	**Today, I am grateful for...**
15:00	
16:00	
17:00	**Today's self care**
18:00	
19:00	
20:00	**Chart your cycle**
21:00	
22:00	
23:00	**Positive affirmation**
Notes	

Thursday | 8 January 2026 - Waning Gibbous

6:00	**Today's quick wins**
7:00	
8:00	
9:00	
10:00	
11:00	**Health and nutrition**
12:00	
13:00	
14:00	**Today, I am grateful for...**
15:00	
16:00	
17:00	**Today's self care**
18:00	
19:00	
20:00	**Chart your cycle**
21:00	
22:00	
23:00	**Positive affirmation**
Notes	

Friday | 9 January 2026 - Waning Gibbous

6:00		Today's quick wins
7:00		
8:00		
9:00		
10:00		
11:00		Health and nutrition
12:00		
13:00		
14:00		Today, I am grateful for...
15:00		
16:00		
17:00		Today's self care
18:00		
19:00		
20:00		Chart your cycle
21:00		
22:00		
23:00		Positive affirmation
Notes		

Saturday | 10 January 2026 - Last Quarter

6:00	**Today's quick wins**
7:00	
8:00	
9:00	
10:00	
11:00	**Health and nutrition**
12:00	
13:00	
14:00	**Today, I am grateful for...**
15:00	
16:00	
17:00	**Today's self care**
18:00	
19:00	
20:00	**Chart your cycle**
21:00	
22:00	
23:00	**Positive affirmation**

Notes

Sunday | 11 January 2026 - Waning Crescent

6:00	Today's quick wins
7:00	
8:00	
9:00	
10:00	
11:00	Health and nutrition
12:00	
13:00	
14:00	Today, I am grateful for...
15:00	
16:00	
17:00	Today's self care
18:00	
19:00	
20:00	Chart your cycle
21:00	
22:00	
23:00	Positive affirmation
Notes	

My Week 12th Jan - 18th Jan

Mon	
Tue	
Wed	
Thu	
Fri	
Sat	
Sun	

Monday | 12 January 2026 - Waning Crescent

6:00	Today's quick wins	
7:00		
8:00		
9:00		
10:00		
11:00	Health and nutrition	
12:00		
13:00		
14:00	Today, I am grateful for…	
15:00		
16:00		
17:00	Today's self care	
18:00		
19:00		
20:00	Chart your cycle	
21:00		
22:00		
23:00	Positive affirmation	
Notes		

Tuesday | 13 January 2026 - Waning Crescent

6:00	Today's quick wins	
7:00		
8:00		
9:00		
10:00		
11:00	Health and nutrition	
12:00		
13:00		
14:00	Today, I am grateful for...	
15:00		
16:00		
17:00	Today's self care	
18:00		
19:00		
20:00	Chart your cycle	
21:00		
22:00		
23:00	Positive affirmation	
Notes		

Wednesday | 14 January 2026 - Waning Crescent

6:00	**Today's quick wins**
7:00	
8:00	
9:00	
10:00	
11:00	**Health and nutrition**
12:00	
13:00	
14:00	**Today, I am grateful for...**
15:00	
16:00	
17:00	**Today's self care**
18:00	
19:00	
20:00	**Chart your cycle**
21:00	
22:00	
23:00	**Positive affirmation**
Notes	

Thursday | 15 January 2026 - Waning Crescent

6:00	Today's quick wins	
7:00		
8:00		
9:00		
10:00		
11:00	Health and nutrition	
12:00		
13:00		
14:00	Today, I am grateful for...	
15:00		
16:00		
17:00	Today's self care	
18:00		
19:00		
20:00	Chart your cycle	
21:00		
22:00		
23:00	Positive affirmation	
Notes		

Friday | 16 January 2026 - Waning Crescent

6:00	**Today's quick wins**
7:00	
8:00	
9:00	
10:00	
11:00	**Health and nutrition**
12:00	
13:00	
14:00	**Today, I am grateful for...**
15:00	
16:00	
17:00	**Today's self care**
18:00	
19:00	
20:00	**Chart your cycle**
21:00	
22:00	
23:00	**Positive affirmation**
Notes	

Saturday | 17 January 2026 - Waning Crescent

6:00	**Today's quick wins**
7:00	
8:00	
9:00	
10:00	
11:00	**Health and nutrition**
12:00	
13:00	
14:00	**Today, I am grateful for...**
15:00	
16:00	
17:00	**Today's self care**
18:00	
19:00	
20:00	**Chart your cycle**
21:00	
22:00	
23:00	**Positive affirmation**
Notes	

Sunday | 18 January 2026 - New Moon in Capricorn 19.51 GMT

6:00	Today's quick wins
7:00	
8:00	
9:00	
10:00	
11:00	Health and nutrition
12:00	
13:00	
14:00	Today, I am grateful for...
15:00	
16:00	
17:00	Today's self care
18:00	
19:00	
20:00	Chart your cycle
21:00	
22:00	
23:00	Positive affirmation
Notes	

My Week 19th Jan - 25th Jan

Mon	
Tue	
Wed	
Thu	
Fri	
Sat	
Sun	

Monday | 19 January 2026 - Waxing Crescent

6:00	**Today's quick wins**
7:00	
8:00	
9:00	
10:00	
11:00	**Health and nutrition**
12:00	
13:00	
14:00	**Today, I am grateful for...**
15:00	
16:00	
17:00	**Today's self care**
18:00	
19:00	
20:00	**Chart your cycle**
21:00	
22:00	
23:00	**Positive affirmation**
Notes	

Tuesday | 20 January 2026 - Waxing Crescent

6:00	Today's quick wins	
7:00		
8:00		
9:00		
10:00		
11:00	Health and nutrition	
12:00		
13:00		
14:00	Today, I am grateful for...	
15:00		
16:00		
17:00	Today's self care	
18:00		
19:00		
20:00	Chart your cycle	
21:00		
22:00		
23:00	Positive affirmation	
Notes		

Wednesday | 21 January 2026 - Waxing Crescent

6:00	Today's quick wins	
7:00		
8:00		
9:00		
10:00		
11:00	Health and nutrition	
12:00		
13:00		
14:00	Today, I am grateful for...	
15:00		
16:00		
17:00	Today's self care	
18:00		
19:00		
20:00	Chart your cycle	
21:00		
22:00		
23:00	Positive affirmation	
Notes		

Thursday | 22 January 2026 - Waxing Crescent

6:00	**Today's quick wins**
7:00	
8:00	
9:00	
10:00	
11:00	**Health and nutrition**
12:00	
13:00	
14:00	**Today, I am grateful for...**
15:00	
16:00	
17:00	**Today's self care**
18:00	
19:00	
20:00	**Chart your cycle**
21:00	
22:00	
23:00	**Positive affirmation**
Notes	

Friday | 23 January 2026 - Waxing Crescent

6:00	**Today's quick wins**
7:00	
8:00	
9:00	
10:00	
11:00	**Health and nutrition**
12:00	
13:00	
14:00	**Today, I am grateful for...**
15:00	
16:00	
17:00	**Today's self care**
18:00	
19:00	
20:00	**Chart your cycle**
21:00	
22:00	
23:00	**Positive affirmation**
Notes	

Saturday | 24 January 2026 - Waxing Crescent

6:00	Today's quick wins
7:00	
8:00	
9:00	
10:00	
11:00	Health and nutrition
12:00	
13:00	
14:00	Today, I am grateful for...
15:00	
16:00	
17:00	Today's self care
18:00	
19:00	
20:00	Chart your cycle
21:00	
22:00	
23:00	Positive affirmation
Notes	

Sunday | 25 January 2026 - Waxing Crescent

6:00	**Today's quick wins**
7:00	
8:00	
9:00	
10:00	
11:00	**Health and nutrition**
12:00	
13:00	
14:00	**Today, I am grateful for...**
15:00	
16:00	
17:00	**Today's self care**
18:00	
19:00	
20:00	**Chart your cycle**
21:00	
22:00	
23:00	**Positive affirmation**
Notes	

My Week 26th Jan - 1st Feb

Mon	
Tue	
Wed	
Thu	
Fri	
Sat	
Sun	

Monday | 26 January 2026 - First Quarter

6:00	**Today's quick wins**
7:00	
8:00	
9:00	
10:00	
11:00	**Health and nutrition**
12:00	
13:00	
14:00	**Today, I am grateful for...**
15:00	
16:00	
17:00	**Today's self care**
18:00	
19:00	
20:00	**Chart your cycle**
21:00	
22:00	
23:00	**Positive affirmation**
Notes	

Tuesday | 27 January 2026 - Waxing Gibbous

6:00	**Today's quick wins**
7:00	
8:00	
9:00	
10:00	
11:00	**Health and nutrition**
12:00	
13:00	
14:00	**Today, I am grateful for...**
15:00	
16:00	
17:00	**Today's self care**
18:00	
19:00	
20:00	**Chart your cycle**
21:00	
22:00	
23:00	**Positive affirmation**
Notes	

Wednesday | 28 January 2026 - Waxing Gibbous

6:00	**Today's quick wins**
7:00	
8:00	
9:00	
10:00	
11:00	**Health and nutrition**
12:00	
13:00	
14:00	**Today, I am grateful for...**
15:00	
16:00	
17:00	**Today's self care**
18:00	
19:00	
20:00	**Chart your cycle**
21:00	
22:00	
23:00	**Positive affirmation**
Notes	

Thursday | 29 January 2026 - Waxing Gibbous

6:00	Today's quick wins
7:00	
8:00	
9:00	
10:00	
11:00	Health and nutrition
12:00	
13:00	
14:00	Today, I am grateful for...
15:00	
16:00	
17:00	Today's self care
18:00	
19:00	
20:00	Chart your cycle
21:00	
22:00	
23:00	Positive affirmation
Notes	

Friday | 30 January 2026 - Waxing Gibbous

6:00	**Today's quick wins**
7:00	
8:00	
9:00	
10:00	
11:00	**Health and nutrition**
12:00	
13:00	
14:00	**Today, I am grateful for...**
15:00	
16:00	
17:00	**Today's self care**
18:00	
19:00	
20:00	**Chart your cycle**
21:00	
22:00	
23:00	**Positive affirmation**
Notes	

Saturday | 31 January 2026 - Waxing Gibbous

6:00		Today's quick wins
7:00		
8:00		
9:00		
10:00		
11:00		Health and nutrition
12:00		
13:00		
14:00		Today, I am grateful for...
15:00		
16:00		
17:00		Today's self care
18:00		
19:00		
20:00		Chart your cycle
21:00		
22:00		
23:00		Positive affirmation
Notes		

January achievements

Be proud of yourself and all that you have achieved this month. Write down your wins, big and small. If you have not achieved everything that you set out to do, that's okay! We learn and grow through our mistakes and experiences. You can use this space to make notes about anything that you have learned.

February 2026

Notes	Monday	Tuesday	Wednesday
	26	27	28
	2	3	4
	9	10	11
	16	17 *Solar Eclipse*	18
	23	24	25

Thursday	Friday	Saturday	Sunday
29	30	31	1 ○
5	6	7	8
12	13	14	15
19	20	21	22
26	27	28	1

February
Lalita Sundari

LALITA

Lalita Sundari is the most beautiful goddess in the Hindu scriptures. She's not here to fight the patriarchy instead she'll seduce it into collapse. She gives us chaos braided in roses.

Her beauty is like divine weaponry. She creates, sustains, and destroys. She's here for our transformation with a body that is literally the cosmos, each part of her form maps the subtle geometry of reality.

Lalita is the heart of Tantra.

Demons never stood a chance. Bhandasura tried to control the world with ignorance and greed. So she winked at him and launched a thousand weapons from her fingertips.

She doesn't demand devotion she simply inspires it, so that once you've seen her, you stop looking outside for divinity. Lalita doesn't come to break the rules,
instead she re-writes the laws of reality.

Crystal: Place *rose quartz* or *rhodonite* at your heart to feel Lalita's love and beauty.

My Vision for February

"Start each day with a positive thought and a grateful heart."

— Roy T. Bennett

Draw, doodle or write about the things that light you up, and let that light ripple out into the world.

Sunday | 1 February 2026 - Full Moon in Leo at 22.08 GMT

6:00	**Today's quick wins**
7:00	
8:00	
9:00	
10:00	
11:00	**Health and nutrition**
12:00	
13:00	
14:00	**Today, I am grateful for...**
15:00	
16:00	
17:00	**Today's self care**
18:00	
19:00	
20:00	**Chart your cycle**
21:00	
22:00	
23:00	**Positive affirmation**
Notes	

My Week 2nd Feb - 8th Feb

Mon	
Tue	
Wed	
Thu	
Fri	
Sat	
Sun	

Monday | 2 February 2026 - Waning Gibbous

6:00	Today's quick wins
7:00	
8:00	
9:00	
10:00	
11:00	Health and nutrition
12:00	
13:00	
14:00	Today, I am grateful for...
15:00	
16:00	
17:00	Today's self care
18:00	
19:00	
20:00	Chart your cycle
21:00	
22:00	
23:00	Positive affirmation
Notes	

Tuesday | 3 February 2026 - Waning Gibbous

6:00	**Today's quick wins**
7:00	
8:00	
9:00	
10:00	
11:00	**Health and nutrition**
12:00	
13:00	
14:00	**Today, I am grateful for...**
15:00	
16:00	
17:00	**Today's self care**
18:00	
19:00	
20:00	**Chart your cycle**
21:00	
22:00	
23:00	**Positive affirmation**

Notes

Wednesday | 4 February 2026 - Waning Gibbous

6:00	**Today's quick wins**
7:00	
8:00	
9:00	
10:00	
11:00	**Health and nutrition**
12:00	
13:00	
14:00	**Today, I am grateful for...**
15:00	
16:00	
17:00	**Today's self care**
18:00	
19:00	
20:00	**Chart your cycle**
21:00	
22:00	
23:00	**Positive affirmation**

Notes

Thursday | 5 February 2026 - Waning Gibbous

6:00		Today's quick wins	
7:00			
8:00			
9:00			
10:00			
11:00		Health and nutrition	
12:00			
13:00			
14:00		Today, I am grateful for...	
15:00			
16:00			
17:00		Today's self care	
18:00			
19:00			
20:00		Chart your cycle	
21:00			
22:00			
23:00		Positive affirmation	
Notes			

Friday | 6 February 2026 - Waning Gibbous

6:00	Today's quick wins	
7:00		
8:00		
9:00		
10:00		
11:00	Health and nutrition	
12:00		
13:00		
14:00	Today, I am grateful for...	
15:00		
16:00		
17:00	Today's self care	
18:00		
19:00		
20:00	Chart your cycle	
21:00		
22:00		
23:00	Positive affirmation	
Notes		

Saturday | 7 February 2026 - Waning Gibbous

6:00		Today's quick wins
7:00		
8:00		
9:00		
10:00		
11:00		Health and nutrition
12:00		
13:00		
14:00		Today, I am grateful for...
15:00		
16:00		
17:00		Today's self care
18:00		
19:00		
20:00		Chart your cycle
21:00		
22:00		
23:00		Positive affirmation
Notes		

Sunday | 8 February 2026 - Waning Gibbous

6:00		Today's quick wins
7:00		
8:00		
9:00		
10:00		
11:00		Health and nutrition
12:00		
13:00		
14:00		Today, I am grateful for...
15:00		
16:00		
17:00		Today's self care
18:00		
19:00		
20:00		Chart your cycle
21:00		
22:00		
23:00		Positive affirmation
Notes		

My Week 9th Feb - 15th Feb

Mon	
Tue	
Wed	
Thu	
Fri	
Sat	
Sun	

Monday | 9 February 2026 - Last Quarter

6:00		Today's quick wins
7:00		
8:00		
9:00		
10:00		
11:00		Health and nutrition
12:00		
13:00		
14:00		Today, I am grateful for...
15:00		
16:00		
17:00		Today's self care
18:00		
19:00		
20:00		Chart your cycle
21:00		
22:00		
23:00		Positive affirmation
Notes		

Tuesday | 10 February 2026 - Waning Crescent

6:00		Today's quick wins
7:00		
8:00		
9:00		
10:00		
11:00		Health and nutrition
12:00		
13:00		
14:00		Today, I am grateful for…
15:00		
16:00		
17:00		Today's self care
18:00		
19:00		
20:00		Chart your cycle
21:00		
22:00		
23:00		Positive affirmation
Notes		

Wednesday | 11 February 2026 - Waning Crescent

6:00	Today's quick wins	
7:00		
8:00		
9:00		
10:00		
11:00	Health and nutrition	
12:00		
13:00		
14:00	Today, I am grateful for...	
15:00		
16:00		
17:00	Today's self care	
18:00		
19:00		
20:00	Chart your cycle	
21:00		
22:00		
23:00	Positive affirmation	
Notes		

Thursday | 12 February 2026 - Waning Crescent

6:00	Today's quick wins	
7:00		
8:00		
9:00		
10:00		
11:00	Health and nutrition	
12:00		
13:00		
14:00	Today, I am grateful for...	
15:00		
16:00		
17:00	Today's self care	
18:00		
19:00		
20:00	Chart your cycle	
21:00		
22:00		
23:00	Positive affirmation	
Notes		

Friday | 13 February 2026 - Waning Crescent

6:00	Today's quick wins	
7:00		
8:00		
9:00		
10:00		
11:00	Health and nutrition	
12:00		
13:00		
14:00	Today, I am grateful for...	
15:00		
16:00		
17:00	Today's self care	
18:00		
19:00		
20:00	Chart your cycle	
21:00		
22:00		
23:00	Positive affirmation	
Notes		

Saturday | 14 February 2026 - Waning Crescent

6:00	**Today's quick wins**
7:00	
8:00	
9:00	
10:00	
11:00	**Health and nutrition**
12:00	
13:00	
14:00	**Today, I am grateful for...**
15:00	
16:00	
17:00	**Today's self care**
18:00	
19:00	
20:00	**Chart your cycle**
21:00	
22:00	
23:00	**Positive affirmation**
Notes	

Sunday | 15 February 2026 - Waning Crescent

6:00	**Today's quick wins**
7:00	
8:00	
9:00	
10:00	
11:00	**Health and nutrition**
12:00	
13:00	
14:00	**Today, I am grateful for...**
15:00	
16:00	
17:00	**Today's self care**
18:00	
19:00	
20:00	**Chart your cycle**
21:00	
22:00	
23:00	**Positive affirmation**
Notes	

My Week 16th Feb - 22nd Feb

Mon	
Tue	
Wed	
Thu	
Fri	
Sat	
Sun	

Monday | 16 February 2026 - Waning Crescent

6:00	**Today's quick wins**	
7:00		
8:00		
9:00		
10:00		
11:00	**Health and nutrition**	
12:00		
13:00		
14:00	**Today, I am grateful for...**	
15:00		
16:00		
17:00	**Today's self care**	
18:00		
19:00		
20:00	**Chart your cycle**	
21:00		
22:00		
23:00	**Positive affirmation**	
Notes		

Tuesday | 17 February 2026 - New Moon Soalr Eclipse in Aquarius at 12.00 GMT

6:00	**Today's quick wins**
7:00	
8:00	
9:00	
10:00	
11:00	**Health and nutrition**
12:00	
13:00	
14:00	**Today, I am grateful for...**
15:00	
16:00	
17:00	**Today's self care**
18:00	
19:00	
20:00	**Chart your cycle**
21:00	
22:00	
23:00	**Positive affirmation**
Notes	

Wednesday | 18 February 2026 - Waxing Crescent

6:00	**Today's quick wins**
7:00	
8:00	
9:00	
10:00	
11:00	**Health and nutrition**
12:00	
13:00	
14:00	**Today, I am grateful for...**
15:00	
16:00	
17:00	**Today's self care**
18:00	
19:00	
20:00	**Chart your cycle**
21:00	
22:00	
23:00	**Positive affirmation**
Notes	

Thursday | 19 February 2026 - Waxing Crescent

6:00	Today's quick wins
7:00	
8:00	
9:00	
10:00	
11:00	Health and nutrition
12:00	
13:00	
14:00	Today, I am grateful for...
15:00	
16:00	
17:00	Today's self care
18:00	
19:00	
20:00	Chart your cycle
21:00	
22:00	
23:00	Positive affirmation

Notes

Friday | 20 February 2026 - Waxing Crescent

6:00	**Today's quick wins**
7:00	
8:00	
9:00	
10:00	
11:00	**Health and nutrition**
12:00	
13:00	
14:00	**Today, I am grateful for...**
15:00	
16:00	
17:00	**Today's self care**
18:00	
19:00	
20:00	**Chart your cycle**
21:00	
22:00	
23:00	**Positive affirmation**
Notes	

Saturday | 21 February 2026 - Waxing Crescent

6:00	**Today's quick wins**
7:00	
8:00	
9:00	
10:00	
11:00	**Health and nutrition**
12:00	
13:00	
14:00	**Today, I am grateful for...**
15:00	
16:00	
17:00	**Today's self care**
18:00	
19:00	
20:00	**Chart your cycle**
21:00	
22:00	
23:00	**Positive affirmation**
Notes	

Sunday | 22 February 2026 - Waxing Crescent

6:00	**Today's quick wins**
7:00	
8:00	
9:00	
10:00	
11:00	**Health and nutrition**
12:00	
13:00	
14:00	**Today, I am grateful for...**
15:00	
16:00	
17:00	**Today's self care**
18:00	
19:00	
20:00	**Chart your cycle**
21:00	
22:00	
23:00	**Positive affirmation**
Notes	

My Week 23rd Feb - 1st Mar

Mon	
Tue	
Wed	
Thu	
Fri	
Sat	
Sun	

Monday | 23 February 2026 - Waxing Crescent

6:00	**Today's quick wins**
7:00	
8:00	
9:00	
10:00	
11:00	**Health and nutrition**
12:00	
13:00	
14:00	**Today, I am grateful for...**
15:00	
16:00	
17:00	**Today's self care**
18:00	
19:00	
20:00	**Chart your cycle**
21:00	
22:00	
23:00	**Positive affirmation**
Notes	

Tuesday | 24 February 2026 - First Quarter

6:00	Today's quick wins
7:00	
8:00	
9:00	
10:00	
11:00	Health and nutrition
12:00	
13:00	
14:00	Today, I am grateful for…
15:00	
16:00	
17:00	Today's self care
18:00	
19:00	
20:00	Chart your cycle
21:00	
22:00	
23:00	Positive affirmation
Notes	

Wednesday | 25 February 2026 - Waxing Gibbous

6:00		Today's quick wins	
7:00			
8:00			
9:00			
10:00			
11:00		Health and nutrition	
12:00			
13:00			
14:00		Today, I am grateful for...	
15:00			
16:00			
17:00		Today's self care	
18:00			
19:00			
20:00		Chart your cycle	
21:00			
22:00			
23:00		Positive affirmation	
Notes			

Thursday | 26 February 2026 - Waxing Gibbous

6:00	Today's quick wins	
7:00		
8:00		
9:00		
10:00		
11:00	Health and nutrition	
12:00		
13:00		
14:00	Today, I am grateful for…	
15:00		
16:00		
17:00	Today's self care	
18:00		
19:00		
20:00	Chart your cycle	
21:00		
22:00		
23:00	Positive affirmation	
Notes		

Friday | 27 February 2026 - Waxing Gibbous

6:00	**Today's quick wins**
7:00	
8:00	
9:00	
10:00	
11:00	**Health and nutrition**
12:00	
13:00	
14:00	**Today, I am grateful for...**
15:00	
16:00	
17:00	**Today's self care**
18:00	
19:00	
20:00	**Chart your cycle**
21:00	
22:00	
23:00	**Positive affirmation**
Notes	

Saturday | 28 February 2026 - Waxing Gibbous

6:00	**Today's quick wins**
7:00	
8:00	
9:00	
10:00	
11:00	**Health and nutrition**
12:00	
13:00	
14:00	**Today, I am grateful for...**
15:00	
16:00	
17:00	**Today's self care**
18:00	
19:00	
20:00	**Chart your cycle**
21:00	
22:00	
23:00	**Positive affirmation**
Notes	

February achievements

Be proud of yourself and all that you have achieved this month. Write down your wins, big and small. If you have not achieved everything that you set out to do, that's okay! We learn and grow through our mistakes and experiences. You can use this space to make notes about anything that you have learned.

March 2026

Notes	Monday	Tuesday	Wednesday
	23	24	25
	2	3 *Lunar Eclipse* ○	4
	9	10	11 ☾
	16	17	18
	23 / 30	24 / 31	25 ☽

Thursday	Friday	Saturday	Sunday
26	27	28	1
5	6	7	8
12	13	14	15
19 ●	20 *Spring Equinox*	21	22
26	27	28	29

March
Persephone

PERSEPHONE

They tried to write her as a victim....but Persephone? She's not a cautionary tale, she's an initiation.
The witch between worlds, daughter of grain and soil. She walks barefoot between sunlight and shadow. Six pomegranate seeds, six sacred vows.
Spring blooms because she allows it. The dead rest because she rules it.
You want light without descent? Joy without grief? Growth without going under? Not with Persephone. She is the hand that guides you down and brings you back whole and transformed.
Her power reminds you that you can die and come back different.
She is the High Witch of Duality, the maiden and the sorceress. She knows what it means to be underestimated, and she knows how to turn that into spellcraft.
Her magic is the cycle itself - the bloom, decay, and return. If you've ever clawed your way back from a winter of the soul, you've already walked her path.
She says:
"Go ahead. Descend."
"Your darkness isn't a flaw. It's a doorway."
"You are not lost. You are becoming."
So gather your bones and your bloodline grief. Set fire to the old story. And follow the Queen down - to be reborn.
Persephone doesn't live in anyone's shadow.
And nor should you.

Crystal: Black obsidian - helps you release fear, confront hidden truths, and feel safe during times of transformation.

My Vision for March

Sunday | 1 March 2026 - Waxing Gibbous

6:00		Today's quick wins
7:00		
8:00		
9:00		
10:00		
11:00		Health and nutrition
12:00		
13:00		
14:00		Today, I am grateful for...
15:00		
16:00		
17:00		Today's self care
18:00		
19:00		
20:00		Chart your cycle
21:00		
22:00		
23:00		Positive affirmation
Notes		

My Week 2nd Mar - 8th Mar

Mon	
Tue	
Wed	
Thu	
Fri	
Sat	
Sun	

Monday | 2 March 2026 - Waxing Gibbous

6:00	Today's quick wins
7:00	
8:00	
9:00	
10:00	
11:00	Health and nutrition
12:00	
13:00	
14:00	Today, I am grateful for…
15:00	
16:00	
17:00	Today's self care
18:00	
19:00	
20:00	Chart your cycle
21:00	
22:00	
23:00	Positive affirmation
Notes	

Tuesday | 3 March 2026 - Full Moon Lunar Eclipse in Virgo at 1.37 GMT

6:00	Today's quick wins
7:00	
8:00	
9:00	
10:00	
11:00	Health and nutrition
12:00	
13:00	
14:00	Today, I am grateful for...
15:00	
16:00	
17:00	Today's self care
18:00	
19:00	
20:00	Chart your cycle
21:00	
22:00	
23:00	Positive affirmation

Notes

Wednesday | 4 March 2026 - Waning Gibbous

6:00		Today's quick wins	
7:00			
8:00			
9:00			
10:00			
11:00		Health and nutrition	
12:00			
13:00			
14:00		Today, I am grateful for...	
15:00			
16:00			
17:00		Today's self care	
18:00			
19:00			
20:00		Chart your cycle	
21:00			
22:00			
23:00		Positive affirmation	
Notes			

Thursday | 5 March 2026 - Waning Gibbous

6:00	Today's quick wins	
7:00		
8:00		
9:00		
10:00		
11:00	Health and nutrition	
12:00		
13:00		
14:00	Today, I am grateful for…	
15:00		
16:00		
17:00	Today's self care	
18:00		
19:00		
20:00	Chart your cycle	
21:00		
22:00		
23:00	Positive affirmation	
Notes		

Friday | 6 March 2026 - Waning Gibbous

6:00	Today's quick wins	
7:00		
8:00		
9:00		
10:00		
11:00	Health and nutrition	
12:00		
13:00		
14:00	Today, I am grateful for…	
15:00		
16:00		
17:00	Today's self care	
18:00		
19:00		
20:00	Chart your cycle	
21:00		
22:00		
23:00	Positive affirmation	
Notes		

Saturday | 7 March 2026 - Waning Gibbous

6:00	**Today's quick wins**
7:00	
8:00	
9:00	
10:00	
11:00	**Health and nutrition**
12:00	
13:00	
14:00	**Today, I am grateful for...**
15:00	
16:00	
17:00	**Today's self care**
18:00	
19:00	
20:00	**Chart your cycle**
21:00	
22:00	
23:00	**Positive affirmation**
Notes	

Sunday | 8 March 2026 - Waning Gibbous

6:00	**Today's quick wins**
7:00	
8:00	
9:00	
10:00	
11:00	**Health and nutrition**
12:00	
13:00	
14:00	**Today, I am grateful for...**
15:00	
16:00	
17:00	**Today's self care**
18:00	
19:00	
20:00	**Chart your cycle**
21:00	
22:00	
23:00	**Positive affirmation**
Notes	

My Week 9th Mar - 15th Mar

Mon	
Tue	
Wed	
Thu	
Fri	
Sat	
Sun	

Monday | 9 March 2026 - Waning Gibbous

6:00	Today's quick wins	
7:00		
8:00		
9:00		
10:00		
11:00	Health and nutrition	
12:00		
13:00		
14:00	Today, I am grateful for…	
15:00		
16:00		
17:00	Today's self care	
18:00		
19:00		
20:00	Chart your cycle	
21:00		
22:00		
23:00	Positive affirmation	
Notes		

Tuesday | 10 March 2026 - Waning Gibbous

6:00	Today's quick wins	
7:00		
8:00		
9:00		
10:00		
11:00	Health and nutrition	
12:00		
13:00		
14:00	Today, I am grateful for...	
15:00		
16:00		
17:00	Today's self care	
18:00		
19:00		
20:00	Chart your cycle	
21:00		
22:00		
23:00	Positive affirmation	
Notes		

Wednesday | 11 March 2026 - Last Quarter

6:00		Today's quick wins
7:00		
8:00		
9:00		
10:00		
11:00		Health and nutrition
12:00		
13:00		
14:00		Today, I am grateful for...
15:00		
16:00		
17:00		Today's self care
18:00		
19:00		
20:00		Chart your cycle
21:00		
22:00		
23:00		Positive affirmation
Notes		

Thursday | 12 March 2026 - Waning Crescent

6:00	Today's quick wins	
7:00		
8:00		
9:00		
10:00		
11:00	Health and nutrition	
12:00		
13:00		
14:00	Today, I am grateful for...	
15:00		
16:00		
17:00	Today's self care	
18:00		
19:00		
20:00	Chart your cycle	
21:00		
22:00		
23:00	Positive affirmation	
Notes		

Friday | 13 March 2026 - Waning Crescent

6:00	**Today's quick wins**
7:00	
8:00	
9:00	
10:00	
11:00	**Health and nutrition**
12:00	
13:00	
14:00	**Today, I am grateful for...**
15:00	
16:00	
17:00	**Today's self care**
18:00	
19:00	
20:00	**Chart your cycle**
21:00	
22:00	
23:00	**Positive affirmation**
Notes	

Saturday | 14 March 2026 - Waning Crescent

6:00	**Today's quick wins**
7:00	
8:00	
9:00	
10:00	
11:00	**Health and nutrition**
12:00	
13:00	
14:00	**Today, I am grateful for...**
15:00	
16:00	
17:00	**Today's self care**
18:00	
19:00	
20:00	**Chart your cycle**
21:00	
22:00	
23:00	**Positive affirmation**
Notes	

Sunday | 15 March 2026 - Waning Crescent

6:00		**Today's quick wins**
7:00		
8:00		
9:00		
10:00		
11:00		**Health and nutrition**
12:00		
13:00		
14:00		**Today, I am grateful for...**
15:00		
16:00		
17:00		**Today's self care**
18:00		
19:00		
20:00		**Chart your cycle**
21:00		
22:00		
23:00		**Positive affirmation**
Notes		

My Week 16th Mar - 22nd Mar

Mon	
Tue	
Wed	
Thu	
Fri	
Sat	
Sun	

Monday | 16 March 2026 - Waning Crescent

6:00	Today's quick wins	
7:00		
8:00		
9:00		
10:00		
11:00	Health and nutrition	
12:00		
13:00		
14:00	Today, I am grateful for...	
15:00		
16:00		
17:00	Today's self care	
18:00		
19:00		
20:00	Chart your cycle	
21:00		
22:00		
23:00	Positive affirmation	
Notes		

Tuesday | 17 March 2026 - Waning Crescent

6:00	Today's quick wins
7:00	
8:00	
9:00	
10:00	
11:00	Health and nutrition
12:00	
13:00	
14:00	Today, I am grateful for...
15:00	
16:00	
17:00	Today's self care
18:00	
19:00	
20:00	Chart your cycle
21:00	
22:00	
23:00	Positive affirmation
Notes	

Wednesday | 18 March 2026 - Waning Crescent

6:00		Today's quick wins	
7:00			
8:00			
9:00			
10:00			
11:00		Health and nutrition	
12:00			
13:00			
14:00		Today, I am grateful for...	
15:00			
16:00			
17:00		Today's self care	
18:00			
19:00			
20:00		Chart your cycle	
21:00			
22:00			
23:00		Positive affirmation	

Notes

Thursday | 19 March 2026 - New Moon in Pisces at 01.23 GMT

6:00		Today's quick wins
7:00		
8:00		
9:00		
10:00		
11:00		Health and nutrition
12:00		
13:00		
14:00		Today, I am grateful for...
15:00		
16:00		
17:00		Today's self care
18:00		
19:00		
20:00		Chart your cycle
21:00		
22:00		
23:00		Positive affirmation

Notes

Friday | 20 March 2026 - Waxing Crescent, Spring Equinox

6:00	**Today's quick wins**
7:00	
8:00	
9:00	
10:00	
11:00	**Health and nutrition**
12:00	
13:00	
14:00	**Today, I am grateful for...**
15:00	
16:00	
17:00	**Today's self care**
18:00	
19:00	
20:00	**Chart your cycle**
21:00	
22:00	
23:00	**Positive affirmation**
Notes	

Saturday | 21 March 2026 - Waxing Crescent

6:00	**Today's quick wins**
7:00	
8:00	
9:00	
10:00	
11:00	**Health and nutrition**
12:00	
13:00	
14:00	**Today, I am grateful for...**
15:00	
16:00	
17:00	**Today's self care**
18:00	
19:00	
20:00	**Chart your cycle**
21:00	
22:00	
23:00	**Positive affirmation**
Notes	

Sunday | 22 March 2026 - Waxing Crescent

6:00		Today's quick wins
7:00		
8:00		
9:00		
10:00		
11:00		Health and nutrition
12:00		
13:00		
14:00		Today, I am grateful for…
15:00		
16:00		
17:00		Today's self care
18:00		
19:00		
20:00		Chart your cycle
21:00		
22:00		
23:00		Positive affirmation
Notes		

My Week 23rd Mar - 29th Mar

Mon	
Tue	
Wed	
Thu	
Fri	
Sat	
Sun	

Monday | 23 March 2026 - Waxing Crescent

6:00	**Today's quick wins**
7:00	
8:00	
9:00	
10:00	
11:00	**Health and nutrition**
12:00	
13:00	
14:00	**Today, I am grateful for...**
15:00	
16:00	
17:00	**Today's self care**
18:00	
19:00	
20:00	**Chart your cycle**
21:00	
22:00	
23:00	**Positive affirmation**

Notes

Tuesday | 24 March 2026 - Waxing Crescent

6:00	**Today's quick wins**
7:00	
8:00	
9:00	
10:00	
11:00	**Health and nutrition**
12:00	
13:00	
14:00	**Today, I am grateful for…**
15:00	
16:00	
17:00	**Today's self care**
18:00	
19:00	
20:00	**Chart your cycle**
21:00	
22:00	
23:00	**Positive affirmation**
Notes	

Wednesday | 25 March 2026 - First Quarter

6:00	**Today's quick wins**
7:00	
8:00	
9:00	
10:00	
11:00	**Health and nutrition**
12:00	
13:00	
14:00	**Today, I am grateful for...**
15:00	
16:00	
17:00	**Today's self care**
18:00	
19:00	
20:00	**Chart your cycle**
21:00	
22:00	
23:00	**Positive affirmation**
Notes	

Thursday | 26 March 2026 - Waxing Gibbous

6:00	Today's quick wins	
7:00		
8:00		
9:00		
10:00		
11:00	Health and nutrition	
12:00		
13:00		
14:00	Today, I am grateful for...	
15:00		
16:00		
17:00	Today's self care	
18:00		
19:00		
20:00	Chart your cycle	
21:00		
22:00		
23:00	Positive affirmation	
Notes		

Friday | 27 March 2026 - Waxing Gibbous

6:00		Today's quick wins	
7:00			
8:00			
9:00			
10:00			
11:00		Health and nutrition	
12:00			
13:00			
14:00		Today, I am grateful for...	
15:00			
16:00			
17:00		Today's self care	
18:00			
19:00			
20:00		Chart your cycle	
21:00			
22:00			
23:00		Positive affirmation	
Notes			

Saturday | 28 March 2026 - Waxing Gibbous

6:00	**Today's quick wins**
7:00	
8:00	
9:00	
10:00	
11:00	**Health and nutrition**
12:00	
13:00	
14:00	**Today, I am grateful for...**
15:00	
16:00	
17:00	**Today's self care**
18:00	
19:00	
20:00	**Chart your cycle**
21:00	
22:00	
23:00	**Positive affirmation**
Notes	

Sunday | 29 March 2026 - Waxing Gibbous

6:00	**Today's quick wins**
7:00	
8:00	
9:00	
10:00	
11:00	**Health and nutrition**
12:00	
13:00	
14:00	**Today, I am grateful for...**
15:00	
16:00	
17:00	**Today's self care**
18:00	
19:00	
20:00	**Chart your cycle**
21:00	
22:00	
23:00	**Positive affirmation**
Notes	

My Week 30th Mar - 5th Apr

Mon	
Tue	
Wed	
Thu	
Fri	
Sat	
Sun	

Monday | 30 March 2026 - Waxing Gibbous

6:00	Today's quick wins
7:00	
8:00	
9:00	
10:00	
11:00	Health and nutrition
12:00	
13:00	
14:00	Today, I am grateful for...
15:00	
16:00	
17:00	Today's self care
18:00	
19:00	
20:00	Chart your cycle
21:00	
22:00	
23:00	Positive affirmation
Notes	

Tuesday | 31 March 2026 - Waxing Gibbous

6:00	Today's quick wins	
7:00		
8:00		
9:00		
10:00		
11:00	Health and nutrition	
12:00		
13:00		
14:00	Today, I am grateful for...	
15:00		
16:00		
17:00	Today's self care	
18:00		
19:00		
20:00	Chart your cycle	
21:00		
22:00		
23:00	Positive affirmation	
Notes		

March achievements

Be proud of yourself and all that you have achieved this month. Write down your wins, big and small. If you have not achieved everything that you set out to do, that's okay! We learn and grow through our mistakes and experiences. You can use this space to make notes about anything that you have learned.

"Nature never hurries,
yet everything is accomplished."

— Lao Tzu

April 2026

Notes	Monday	Tuesday	Wednesday
	30	31	1
	6	7	8
	13	14	15
	20	21	22
	27	28	29

Thursday	Friday	Saturday	Sunday
2 ○	3	4	5
9	10 ☽	11	12
16	17 ●	18	19
23	24 ☾	25	26
30			

April
Green Tara

GREEN TARA

Green Tara is a goddess of compassion who protects us from danger.

She's the hand outstretched just as you're slipping. Tara walks with you, already halfway through the door you thought was locked.

Born from the tears of Avalokiteshvara, the Bodhisattva of Infinite Compassion, Green Tara is the action in the face of suffering. She doesnt just show empathy, but has the guts to move with it. She's known as "She Who Saves".

Her mantra, "Om Tare Tuttare Ture Soha," is like a spell of courage.
Tara has 21 faces, but Green Tara is the quick one. Think of her not as some distant deity, but the part of you that refuses to give up.
The goddess in your resilience.

Next time the path is dark, call her name. Because Green Tara isn't just a figure in a thangka - she's the rebel queen already running beside you.

Crystal: Jade - a sacred stone in many spiritual traditions as it carries vibrations of harmony, protection, and good fortune all of which align beautifully with Tara's protective and benevolent qualities. Keep it on your altar or wear as a talisman when invoking her blessings.

My Vision for April

Wednesday | 1 April 2026 - Waxing Gibbous

6:00	**Today's quick wins**
7:00	
8:00	
9:00	
10:00	
11:00	**Health and nutrition**
12:00	
13:00	
14:00	**Today, I am grateful for...**
15:00	
16:00	
17:00	**Today's self care**
18:00	
19:00	
20:00	**Chart your cycle**
21:00	
22:00	
23:00	**Positive affirmation**
Notes	

Thursday | 2 April 2026 - Full Moon in Libra at 02.11 GMT

6:00	**Today's quick wins**
7:00	
8:00	
9:00	
10:00	
11:00	**Health and nutrition**
12:00	
13:00	
14:00	**Today, I am grateful for...**
15:00	
16:00	
17:00	**Today's self care**
18:00	
19:00	
20:00	**Chart your cycle**
21:00	
22:00	
23:00	**Positive affirmation**
Notes	

Friday | 3 April 2026 - Waning Gibbous

6:00		Today's quick wins
7:00		
8:00		
9:00		
10:00		
11:00		Health and nutrition
12:00		
13:00		
14:00		Today, I am grateful for...
15:00		
16:00		
17:00		Today's self care
18:00		
19:00		
20:00		Chart your cycle
21:00		
22:00		
23:00		Positive affirmation
Notes		

Saturday | 4 April 2026 - Waning Gibbous

6:00	**Today's quick wins**
7:00	
8:00	
9:00	
10:00	
11:00	**Health and nutrition**
12:00	
13:00	
14:00	**Today, I am grateful for...**
15:00	
16:00	
17:00	**Today's self care**
18:00	
19:00	
20:00	**Chart your cycle**
21:00	
22:00	
23:00	**Positive affirmation**
Notes	

Sunday | 5 April 2026 - Waning Gibbous

6:00		Today's quick wins	
7:00			
8:00			
9:00			
10:00			
11:00		Health and nutrition	
12:00			
13:00			
14:00		Today, I am grateful for...	
15:00			
16:00			
17:00		Today's self care	
18:00			
19:00			
20:00		Chart your cycle	
21:00			
22:00			
23:00		Positive affirmation	
Notes			

My Week 6th Apr - 12th Apr

Mon	
Tue	
Wed	
Thu	
Fri	
Sat	
Sun	

Monday | 6 April 2026 - Waning Gibbous

6:00	**Today's quick wins**
7:00	
8:00	
9:00	
10:00	
11:00	**Health and nutrition**
12:00	
13:00	
14:00	**Today, I am grateful for...**
15:00	
16:00	
17:00	**Today's self care**
18:00	
19:00	
20:00	**Chart your cycle**
21:00	
22:00	
23:00	**Positive affirmation**
Notes	

Tuesday | 7 April 2026 - Waning Gibbous

6:00	Today's quick wins	
7:00		
8:00		
9:00		
10:00		
11:00	Health and nutrition	
12:00		
13:00		
14:00	Today, I am grateful for...	
15:00		
16:00		
17:00	Today's self care	
18:00		
19:00		
20:00	Chart your cycle	
21:00		
22:00		
23:00	Positive affirmation	
Notes		

Wednesday | 8 April 2026 - Waning Gibbous

6:00	**Today's quick wins**
7:00	
8:00	
9:00	
10:00	
11:00	**Health and nutrition**
12:00	
13:00	
14:00	**Today, I am grateful for…**
15:00	
16:00	
17:00	**Today's self care**
18:00	
19:00	
20:00	**Chart your cycle**
21:00	
22:00	
23:00	**Positive affirmation**
Notes	

Thursday | 9 April 2026 - Waning Gibbous

6:00	**Today's quick wins**
7:00	
8:00	
9:00	
10:00	
11:00	**Health and nutrition**
12:00	
13:00	
14:00	**Today, I am grateful for...**
15:00	
16:00	
17:00	**Today's self care**
18:00	
19:00	
20:00	**Chart your cycle**
21:00	
22:00	
23:00	**Positive affirmation**
Notes	

Friday | 10 April 2026 - Last Quarter

6:00	**Today's quick wins**
7:00	
8:00	
9:00	
10:00	
11:00	**Health and nutrition**
12:00	
13:00	
14:00	**Today, I am grateful for...**
15:00	
16:00	
17:00	**Today's self care**
18:00	
19:00	
20:00	**Chart your cycle**
21:00	
22:00	
23:00	**Positive affirmation**
Notes	

Saturday | 11 April 2026 - Waning Crescent

6:00	**Today's quick wins**	
7:00		
8:00		
9:00		
10:00		
11:00	**Health and nutrition**	
12:00		
13:00		
14:00	**Today, I am grateful for...**	
15:00		
16:00		
17:00	**Today's self care**	
18:00		
19:00		
20:00	**Chart your cycle**	
21:00		
22:00		
23:00	**Positive affirmation**	
Notes		

Sunday | 12 April 2026 - Waning Crescent

6:00	**Today's quick wins**
7:00	
8:00	
9:00	
10:00	
11:00	**Health and nutrition**
12:00	
13:00	
14:00	**Today, I am grateful for...**
15:00	
16:00	
17:00	**Today's self care**
18:00	
19:00	
20:00	**Chart your cycle**
21:00	
22:00	
23:00	**Positive affirmation**
Notes	

My Week 13th Apr – 19th Apr

Mon	
Tue	
Wed	
Thu.	
Fri	
Sat	
Sun	

Monday | 13 April 2026 - Waning Crescent

6:00		Today's quick wins
7:00		
8:00		
9:00		
10:00		
11:00		Health and nutrition
12:00		
13:00		
14:00		Today, I am grateful for...
15:00		
16:00		
17:00		Today's self care
18:00		
19:00		
20:00		Chart your cycle
21:00		
22:00		
23:00		Positive affirmation
Notes		

Tuesday | 14 April 2026 - Waning Crescent

6:00	Today's quick wins	
7:00		
8:00		
9:00		
10:00		
11:00	Health and nutrition	
12:00		
13:00		
14:00	Today, I am grateful for...	
15:00		
16:00		
17:00	Today's self care	
18:00		
19:00		
20:00	Chart your cycle	
21:00		
22:00		
23:00	Positive affirmation	
Notes		

Wednesday | 15 April 2026 - Waning Crescent

6:00	Today's quick wins	
7:00		
8:00		
9:00		
10:00		
11:00	Health and nutrition	
12:00		
13:00		
14:00	Today, I am grateful for…	
15:00		
16:00		
17:00	Today's self care	
18:00		
19:00		
20:00	Chart your cycle	
21:00		
22:00		
23:00	Positive affirmation	
Notes		

Thursday | 16 April 2026 - Waning Crescent

6:00	**Today's quick wins**
7:00	
8:00	
9:00	
10:00	
11:00	**Health and nutrition**
12:00	
13:00	
14:00	**Today, I am grateful for…**
15:00	
16:00	
17:00	**Today's self care**
18:00	
19:00	
20:00	**Chart your cycle**
21:00	
22:00	
23:00	**Positive affirmation**
Notes	

Friday | 17 April 2026 - New Moon in Aries at 11.51 GMT

6:00	Today's quick wins	
7:00		
8:00		
9:00		
10:00		
11:00	Health and nutrition	
12:00		
13:00		
14:00	Today, I am grateful for...	
15:00		
16:00		
17:00	Today's self care	
18:00		
19:00		
20:00	Chart your cycle	
21:00		
22:00		
23:00	Positive affirmation	
Notes		

Saturday | 18 April 2026 - Waxing Crescent

6:00	**Today's quick wins**
7:00	
8:00	
9:00	
10:00	
11:00	**Health and nutrition**
12:00	
13:00	
14:00	**Today, I am grateful for…**
15:00	
16:00	
17:00	**Today's self care**
18:00	
19:00	
20:00	**Chart your cycle**
21:00	
22:00	
23:00	**Positive affirmation**
Notes	

Sunday | 19 April 2026 - Waxing Crescent

6:00	Today's quick wins
7:00	
8:00	
9:00	
10:00	
11:00	Health and nutrition
12:00	
13:00	
14:00	Today, I am grateful for...
15:00	
16:00	
17:00	Today's self care
18:00	
19:00	
20:00	Chart your cycle
21:00	
22:00	
23:00	Positive affirmation
Notes	

My Week 20th Apr - 26th - Apr

Mon	
Tue	
Wed	
Thu	
Fri	
Sat	
Sun	

Monday | 20 April 2026 - Waxing Crescent

6:00		Today's quick wins
7:00		
8:00		
9:00		
10:00		
11:00		Health and nutrition
12:00		
13:00		
14:00		Today, I am grateful for...
15:00		
16:00		
17:00		Today's self care
18:00		
19:00		
20:00		Chart your cycle
21:00		
22:00		
23:00		Positive affirmation
Notes		

Tuesday | 21 April 2026 - Waxing Crescent

6:00	**Today's quick wins**
7:00	
8:00	
9:00	
10:00	
11:00	**Health and nutrition**
12:00	
13:00	
14:00	**Today, I am grateful for...**
15:00	
16:00	
17:00	**Today's self care**
18:00	
19:00	
20:00	**Chart your cycle**
21:00	
22:00	
23:00	**Positive affirmation**
Notes	

Wednesday | 22 April 2026 - Waxing Crescent

6:00	**Today's quick wins**
7:00	
8:00	
9:00	
10:00	
11:00	**Health and nutrition**
12:00	
13:00	
14:00	**Today, I am grateful for...**
15:00	
16:00	
17:00	**Today's self care**
18:00	
19:00	
20:00	**Chart your cycle**
21:00	
22:00	
23:00	**Positive affirmation**
Notes	

Thursday | 23 April 2026 - Waxing Crescent

6:00	**Today's quick wins**
7:00	
8:00	
9:00	
10:00	
11:00	**Health and nutrition**
12:00	
13:00	
14:00	**Today, I am grateful for...**
15:00	
16:00	
17:00	**Today's self care**
18:00	
19:00	
20:00	**Chart your cycle**
21:00	
22:00	
23:00	**Positive affirmation**
Notes	

Friday | 24 April 2026 - First Quarter

6:00	Today's quick wins
7:00	
8:00	
9:00	
10:00	
11:00	Health and nutrition
12:00	
13:00	
14:00	Today, I am grateful for...
15:00	
16:00	
17:00	Today's self care
18:00	
19:00	
20:00	Chart your cycle
21:00	
22:00	
23:00	Positive affirmation
Notes	

Saturday | 25 April 2026 - Waxing Gibbous

6:00		**Today's quick wins**
7:00		
8:00		
9:00		
10:00		
11:00		**Health and nutrition**
12:00		
13:00		
14:00		**Today, I am grateful for...**
15:00		
16:00		
17:00		**Today's self care**
18:00		
19:00		
20:00		**Chart your cycle**
21:00		
22:00		
23:00		**Positive affirmation**
Notes		

Sunday | 26 April 2026 - Waxing Gibbous

6:00	Today's quick wins	
7:00		
8:00		
9:00		
10:00		
11:00	Health and nutrition	
12:00		
13:00		
14:00	Today, I am grateful for...	
15:00		
16:00		
17:00	Today's self care	
18:00		
19:00		
20:00	Chart your cycle	
21:00		
22:00		
23:00	Positive affirmation	
Notes		

My Week 27th Apr - 3rd May

Mon	
Tue	
Wed	
Thu	
Fri	
Sat	
Sun	

Monday | 27 April 2026 - Waxing Gibbous

6:00	**Today's quick wins**
7:00	
8:00	
9:00	
10:00	
11:00	**Health and nutrition**
12:00	
13:00	
14:00	**Today, I am grateful for...**
15:00	
16:00	
17:00	**Today's self care**
18:00	
19:00	
20:00	**Chart your cycle**
21:00	
22:00	
23:00	**Positive affirmation**
Notes	

Tuesday | 28 April 2026 - Waxing Gibbous

6:00	**Today's quick wins**
7:00	
8:00	
9:00	
10:00	
11:00	**Health and nutrition**
12:00	
13:00	
14:00	**Today, I am grateful for...**
15:00	
16:00	
17:00	**Today's self care**
18:00	
19:00	
20:00	**Chart your cycle**
21:00	
22:00	
23:00	**Positive affirmation**
Notes	

Wednesday | 29 April 2026 - Waxing Gibbous

6:00	Today's quick wins
7:00	
8:00	
9:00	
10:00	
11:00	Health and nutrition
12:00	
13:00	
14:00	Today, I am grateful for...
15:00	
16:00	
17:00	Today's self care
18:00	
19:00	
20:00	Chart your cycle
21:00	
22:00	
23:00	Positive affirmation
Notes	

Thursday | 30 April 2026 - Waxing Gibbous

6:00		**Today's quick wins**	
7:00			
8:00			
9:00			
10:00			
11:00		**Health and nutrition**	
12:00			
13:00			
14:00		**Today, I am grateful for...**	
15:00			
16:00			
17:00		**Today's self care**	
18:00			
19:00			
20:00		**Chart your cycle**	
21:00			
22:00			
23:00		**Positive affirmation**	
Notes			

April achievements

Be proud of yourself and all that you have achieved this month. Write down your wins, big and small. If you have not achieved everything that you set out to do, that's okay! We learn and grow through our mistakes and experiences. You can use this space to make notes about anything that you have learned.

"Your thoughts become things."
— Rhonda Byrne, The Secret

May 2026

Notes	Monday	Tuesday	Wednesday
	4	5	6
	11	12	13
	18	19	20
	25	26	27

Thursday	Friday	Saturday	Sunday
30	1 ○	2	3
7	8	9 ☾	10
14	15	16 ●	17
21	22	23 ☽	24
28	29	30	31 ○

May
Goddess Freyja

FREYJA

Freyja, The Gold-Blooded Witch of Love and War
She is the Norse goddess of love, but hers is the kind that burns things clean.

She rides a chariot pulled by cats, draped in falcon feathers, deciding which warriors rise and which fall. She's not waiting for Odin's approval. She gets first pick of the dead because half of Valhalla belongs to her.

Goddess of love, sorcery, sovereignty, and the silver-threaded mysteries, she is the Völva Queen - mistress of Seiðr, the kind of magic that shifts fate itself. They feared her power, so they tried to shame it. Called her names. Branded her a witch. She wore the gold necklace (Brísingamen) anyway.

Freyja is the part of you that knows your worth in a room that wants you to forget.

Freyja doesn't need your obedience, she wants your liberation. So love like it's sacred and cast spells like your ancestors are watching. Freyja never bowed to anyone.

Crystal: Amber - the ancient Wisdom, warmth & protection in this stone is deeply connected to Norse traditions, as amber was sacred to Freyja herself.

My Vision for May

Friday | 1 May 2026 - Full Moon in Scorpio at 17.22 GMT

6:00		Today's quick wins
7:00		
8:00		
9:00		
10:00		
11:00		Health and nutrition
12:00		
13:00		
14:00		Today, I am grateful for...
15:00		
16:00		
17:00		Today's self care
18:00		
19:00		
20:00		Chart your cycle
21:00		
22:00		
23:00		Positive affirmation
Notes		

Saturday | 2 May 2026 - Waning Gibbous

6:00	Today's quick wins	
7:00		
8:00		
9:00		
10:00		
11:00	Health and nutrition	
12:00		
13:00		
14:00	Today, I am grateful for...	
15:00		
16:00		
17:00	Today's self care	
18:00		
19:00		
20:00	Chart your cycle	
21:00		
22:00		
23:00	Positive affirmation	
Notes		

Sunday | 3 May 2026 - Waning Gibbous

6:00	Today's quick wins
7:00	
8:00	
9:00	
10:00	
11:00	Health and nutrition
12:00	
13:00	
14:00	Today, I am grateful for…
15:00	
16:00	
17:00	Today's self care
18:00	
19:00	
20:00	Chart your cycle
21:00	
22:00	
23:00	Positive affirmation
Notes	

My Week 4th May – 10th May

Mon	
Tue	
Wed	
Thu	
Fri	
Sat	
Sun	

Monday | 4 May 2026 - Waning Gibbous

6:00	Today's quick wins
7:00	
8:00	
9:00	
10:00	
11:00	Health and nutrition
12:00	
13:00	
14:00	Today, I am grateful for…
15:00	
16:00	
17:00	Today's self care
18:00	
19:00	
20:00	Chart your cycle
21:00	
22:00	
23:00	Positive affirmation
Notes	

Tuesday | 5 May 2026 - Waning Gibbous

6:00	Today's quick wins	
7:00		
8:00		
9:00		
10:00		
11:00	Health and nutrition	
12:00		
13:00		
14:00	Today, I am grateful for...	
15:00		
16:00		
17:00	Today's self care	
18:00		
19:00		
20:00	Chart your cycle	
21:00		
22:00		
23:00	Positive affirmation	
Notes		

Wednesday | 6 May 2026 - Waning Gibbous

6:00		Today's quick wins	
7:00			
8:00			
9:00			
10:00			
11:00		Health and nutrition	
12:00			
13:00			
14:00		Today, I am grateful for...	
15:00			
16:00			
17:00		Today's self care	
18:00			
19:00			
20:00		Chart your cycle	
21:00			
22:00			
23:00		Positive affirmation	
Notes			

Thursday | 7 May 2026 - Waning Gibbous

6:00	**Today's quick wins**
7:00	
8:00	
9:00	
10:00	
11:00	**Health and nutrition**
12:00	
13:00	
14:00	**Today, I am grateful for...**
15:00	
16:00	
17:00	**Today's self care**
18:00	
19:00	
20:00	**Chart your cycle**
21:00	
22:00	
23:00	**Positive affirmation**
Notes	

Friday	8 May 2026 - Waning Gibbous
6:00	Today's quick wins
7:00	
8:00	
9:00	
10:00	
11:00	Health and nutrition
12:00	
13:00	
14:00	Today, I am grateful for...
15:00	
16:00	
17:00	Today's self care
18:00	
19:00	
20:00	Chart your cycle
21:00	
22:00	
23:00	Positive affirmation
Notes	

Saturday | 9 May 2026 - Last Quarter

6:00	Today's quick wins	
7:00		
8:00		
9:00		
10:00		
11:00	Health and nutrition	
12:00		
13:00		
14:00	Today, I am grateful for...	
15:00		
16:00		
17:00	Today's self care	
18:00		
19:00		
20:00	Chart your cycle	
21:00		
22:00		
23:00	Positive affirmation	
Notes		

Sunday | 10 May 2026 - Last Quarter

6:00	Today's quick wins
7:00	
8:00	
9:00	
10:00	
11:00	Health and nutrition
12:00	
13:00	
14:00	Today, I am grateful for…
15:00	
16:00	
17:00	Today's self care
18:00	
19:00	
20:00	Chart your cycle
21:00	
22:00	
23:00	Positive affirmation
Notes	

My Week 14th May - 17th May

Mon	
Tue	
Wed	
Thu	
Fri	
Sat	
Sun	

Monday | 11 May 2026 - Waning Crescent

6:00	Today's quick wins	
7:00		
8:00		
9:00		
10:00		
11:00	Health and nutrition	
12:00		
13:00		
14:00	Today, I am grateful for...	
15:00		
16:00		
17:00	Today's self care	
18:00		
19:00		
20:00	Chart your cycle	
21:00		
22:00		
23:00	Positive affirmation	
Notes		

Tuesday | 12 May 2026 - Waning Crescent

6:00	**Today's quick wins**
7:00	
8:00	
9:00	
10:00	
11:00	**Health and nutrition**
12:00	
13:00	
14:00	**Today, I am grateful for...**
15:00	
16:00	
17:00	**Today's self care**
18:00	
19:00	
20:00	**Chart your cycle**
21:00	
22:00	
23:00	**Positive affirmation**
Notes	

Wednesday | 13 May 2026 - Waning Crescent

6:00	**Today's quick wins**	
7:00		
8:00		
9:00		
10:00		
11:00	**Health and nutrition**	
12:00		
13:00		
14:00	**Today, I am grateful for...**	
15:00		
16:00		
17:00	**Today's self care**	
18:00		
19:00		
20:00	**Chart your cycle**	
21:00		
22:00		
23:00	**Positive affirmation**	
Notes		

Thursday | 14 May 2026 - Waning Crescent

6:00	Today's quick wins	
7:00		
8:00		
9:00		
10:00		
11:00	Health and nutrition	
12:00		
13:00		
14:00	Today, I am grateful for...	
15:00		
16:00		
17:00	Today's self care	
18:00		
19:00		
20:00	Chart your cycle	
21:00		
22:00		
23:00	Positive affirmation	
Notes		

Friday | 15 May 2026 - Waning Crescent

6:00		Today's quick wins
7:00		
8:00		
9:00		
10:00		
11:00		Health and nutrition
12:00		
13:00		
14:00		Today, I am grateful for...
15:00		
16:00		
17:00		Today's self care
18:00		
19:00		
20:00		Chart your cycle
21:00		
22:00		
23:00		Positive affirmation
Notes		

Saturday | 16 May 2026 - New Moon in Taurus at 20.00 GMT

6:00	**Today's quick wins**
7:00	
8:00	
9:00	
10:00	
11:00	**Health and nutrition**
12:00	
13:00	
14:00	**Today, I am grateful for...**
15:00	
16:00	
17:00	**Today's self care**
18:00	
19:00	
20:00	**Chart your cycle**
21:00	
22:00	
23:00	**Positive affirmation**
Notes	

Sunday | 17 May 2026 - Waxing Crescent

6:00		**Today's quick wins**
7:00		
8:00		
9:00		
10:00		
11:00		**Health and nutrition**
12:00		
13:00		
14:00		**Today, I am grateful for...**
15:00		
16:00		
17:00		**Today's self care**
18:00		
19:00		
20:00		**Chart your cycle**
21:00		
22:00		
23:00		**Positive affirmation**
Notes		

My Week 18th May - 24th May

Mon	
Tue	
Wed	
Thu	
Fri	
Sat	
Sun	

Monday | 18 May 2026 - Waxing Crescent

6:00	Today's quick wins	
7:00		
8:00		
9:00		
10:00		
11:00	Health and nutrition	
12:00		
13:00		
14:00	Today, I am grateful for...	
15:00		
16:00		
17:00	Today's self care	
18:00		
19:00		
20:00	Chart your cycle	
21:00		
22:00		
23:00	Positive affirmation	
Notes		

Tuesday | 19 May 2026 - Waxing Crescent

6:00		Today's quick wins	
7:00			
8:00			
9:00			
10:00			
11:00		Health and nutrition	
12:00			
13:00			
14:00		Today, I am grateful for...	
15:00			
16:00			
17:00		Today's self care	
18:00			
19:00			
20:00		Chart your cycle	
21:00			
22:00			
23:00		Positive affirmation	
Notes			

Wednesday | 20 May 2026 - Waxing Crescent

6:00	Today's quick wins
7:00	
8:00	
9:00	
10:00	
11:00	Health and nutrition
12:00	
13:00	
14:00	Today, I am grateful for...
15:00	
16:00	
17:00	Today's self care
18:00	
19:00	
20:00	Chart your cycle
21:00	
22:00	
23:00	Positive affirmation
Notes	

Thursday | 21 May 2026 - Waxing Crescent

6:00	**Today's quick wins**
7:00	
8:00	
9:00	
10:00	
11:00	**Health and nutrition**
12:00	
13:00	
14:00	**Today, I am grateful for...**
15:00	
16:00	
17:00	**Today's self care**
18:00	
19:00	
20:00	**Chart your cycle**
21:00	
22:00	
23:00	**Positive affirmation**

Notes

Friday | 22 May 2026 - Waxing Crescent

6:00	**Today's quick wins**
7:00	
8:00	
9:00	
10:00	
11:00	**Health and nutrition**
12:00	
13:00	
14:00	**Today, I am grateful for…**
15:00	
16:00	
17:00	**Today's self care**
18:00	
19:00	
20:00	**Chart your cycle**
21:00	
22:00	
23:00	**Positive affirmation**
Notes	

Saturday | 23 May 2026 - First Quarter

6:00	**Today's quick wins**
7:00	
8:00	
9:00	
10:00	
11:00	**Health and nutrition**
12:00	
13:00	
14:00	**Today, I am grateful for...**
15:00	
16:00	
17:00	**Today's self care**
18:00	
19:00	
20:00	**Chart your cycle**
21:00	
22:00	
23:00	**Positive affirmation**
Notes	

Sunday | 24 May 2026 - Waxing Gibbous

6:00	**Today's quick wins**
7:00	
8:00	
9:00	
10:00	
11:00	**Health and nutrition**
12:00	
13:00	
14:00	**Today, I am grateful for...**
15:00	
16:00	
17:00	**Today's self care**
18:00	
19:00	
20:00	**Chart your cycle**
21:00	
22:00	
23:00	**Positive affirmation**
Notes	

My Week 25th May – 31st May

Mon	
Tue	
Wed	
Thu	
Fri	
Sat	
Sun	

Monday | 25 May 2026 - Waxing Gibbous

6:00	Today's quick wins	
7:00		
8:00		
9:00		
10:00		
11:00	Health and nutrition	
12:00		
13:00		
14:00	Today, I am grateful for...	
15:00		
16:00		
17:00	Today's self care	
18:00		
19:00		
20:00	Chart your cycle	
21:00		
22:00		
23:00	Positive affirmation	
Notes		

Tuesday | 26 May 2026 - Waxing Gibbous

6:00	Today's quick wins
7:00	
8:00	
9:00	
10:00	
11:00	Health and nutrition
12:00	
13:00	
14:00	Today, I am grateful for...
15:00	
16:00	
17:00	Today's self care
18:00	
19:00	
20:00	Chart your cycle
21:00	
22:00	
23:00	Positive affirmation
Notes	

Wednesday | 27 May 2026 - Waxing Gibbous

6:00		Today's quick wins
7:00		
8:00		
9:00		
10:00		
11:00		Health and nutrition
12:00		
13:00		
14:00		Today, I am grateful for...
15:00		
16:00		
17:00		Today's self care
18:00		
19:00		
20:00		Chart your cycle
21:00		
22:00		
23:00		Positive affirmation
Notes		

Thursday | 28 May 2026 - Waxing Gibbous

6:00	**Today's quick wins**
7:00	
8:00	
9:00	
10:00	
11:00	**Health and nutrition**
12:00	
13:00	
14:00	**Today, I am grateful for...**
15:00	
16:00	
17:00	**Today's self care**
18:00	
19:00	
20:00	**Chart your cycle**
21:00	
22:00	
23:00	**Positive affirmation**

Notes

Friday | 29 May 2026 - Waxing Gibbous

6:00		Today's quick wins
7:00		
8:00		
9:00		
10:00		
11:00		Health and nutrition
12:00		
13:00		
14:00		Today, I am grateful for...
15:00		
16:00		
17:00		Today's self care
18:00		
19:00		
20:00		Chart your cycle
21:00		
22:00		
23:00		Positive affirmation
Notes		

Saturday | 30 May 2026 - Waxing Gibbous

6:00	Today's quick wins
7:00	
8:00	
9:00	
10:00	
11:00	Health and nutrition
12:00	
13:00	
14:00	Today, I am grateful for...
15:00	
16:00	
17:00	Today's self care
18:00	
19:00	
20:00	Chart your cycle
21:00	
22:00	
23:00	Positive affirmation
Notes	

Sunday | 31 May 2026 - Full Moon in Sagittarius at 08.44 GMT

6:00	**Today's quick wins**
7:00	
8:00	
9:00	
10:00	
11:00	**Health and nutrition**
12:00	
13:00	
14:00	**Today, I am grateful for...**
15:00	
16:00	
17:00	**Today's self care**
18:00	
19:00	
20:00	**Chart your cycle**
21:00	
22:00	
23:00	**Positive affirmation**
Notes	

May achievements

Be proud of yourself and all that you have achieved this month. Write down your wins, big and small. If you have not achieved everything that you set out to do, that's okay! We learn and grow through our mistakes and experiences. You can use this space to make notes about anything that you have learned.

June 2026

Notes	Monday	Tuesday	Wednesday
	1	2	3
	8 ☽	9	10
	15 ●	16	17
	22 ☾	23	24
	29 ○	30	

Thursday	Friday	Saturday	Sunday
4	5	6	7
11	12	13	14
18	19	20	21 *Summer Solstice*
25	26	27	28

June
Atalanta

ATALANTA

Atalanta wasn't born to sit still and smile pretty, she was born in the wild. Left on a mountaintop to die because her father wanted a son. But the bears raised her and she grew up on instinct.

Fast-forward a few years and she's outrunning every man in Greece, bow on her back, freedom in her veins. While the other girls were being taught how to submit, Atalanta was wrestling centaurs.

She took an oath of no men, marriage or chains. If you wanted her hand, you had to beat her in a footrace, but she was faster than the gods. And all who tried to win her ended up face-down in the dirt.

Atalanta was never about taming the beast. She was the beast. She's here to remind you about freedom, strength and power - however that looks to you.

Crystal: Carnelian - Use during physical training or any challenge that requires courage and stamina.

My Vision for June

My Week 1st Jun – 7th Jun

Mon	
Tue	
Wed	
Thu	
Fri	
Sat	
Sun	

Monday | 1 June 2026 - Waning Gibbous

6:00	**Today's quick wins**
7:00	
8:00	
9:00	
10:00	
11:00	**Health and nutrition**
12:00	
13:00	
14:00	**Today, I am grateful for...**
15:00	
16:00	
17:00	**Today's self care**
18:00	
19:00	
20:00	**Chart your cycle**
21:00	
22:00	
23:00	**Positive affirmation**
Notes	

Tuesday | 2 June 2026 - Waning Gibbous

6:00	Today's quick wins
7:00	
8:00	
9:00	
10:00	
11:00	Health and nutrition
12:00	
13:00	
14:00	Today, I am grateful for...
15:00	
16:00	
17:00	Today's self care
18:00	
19:00	
20:00	Chart your cycle
21:00	
22:00	
23:00	Positive affirmation
Notes	

Wednesday | 3 June 2026 - Waning Gibbous

6:00		Today's quick wins
7:00		
8:00		
9:00		
10:00		
11:00		Health and nutrition
12:00		
13:00		
14:00		Today, I am grateful for…
15:00		
16:00		
17:00		Today's self care
18:00		
19:00		
20:00		Chart your cycle
21:00		
22:00		
23:00		Positive affirmation
Notes		

Thursday | 4 June 2026 - Waning Gibbous

6:00	**Today's quick wins**
7:00	
8:00	
9:00	
10:00	
11:00	**Health and nutrition**
12:00	
13:00	
14:00	**Today, I am grateful for...**
15:00	
16:00	
17:00	**Today's self care**
18:00	
19:00	
20:00	**Chart your cycle**
21:00	
22:00	
23:00	**Positive affirmation**

Notes

Friday | 5 June 2026 - Waning Gibbous

6:00	Today's quick wins	
7:00		
8:00		
9:00		
10:00		
11:00	Health and nutrition	
12:00		
13:00		
14:00	Today, I am grateful for...	
15:00		
16:00		
17:00	Today's self care	
18:00		
19:00		
20:00	Chart your cycle	
21:00		
22:00		
23:00	Positive affirmation	
Notes		

Saturday | 6 June 2026 - Waning Gibbous

6:00	**Today's quick wins**
7:00	
8:00	
9:00	
10:00	
11:00	**Health and nutrition**
12:00	
13:00	
14:00	**Today, I am grateful for...**
15:00	
16:00	
17:00	**Today's self care**
18:00	
19:00	
20:00	**Chart your cycle**
21:00	
22:00	
23:00	**Positive affirmation**
Notes	

Sunday | 7 June 2026 - Waning Gibbous

6:00	**Today's quick wins**
7:00	
8:00	
9:00	
10:00	
11:00	**Health and nutrition**
12:00	
13:00	
14:00	**Today, I am grateful for...**
15:00	
16:00	
17:00	**Today's self care**
18:00	
19:00	
20:00	**Chart your cycle**
21:00	
22:00	
23:00	**Positive affirmation**
Notes	

My Week 8th Jun - 14th Jun

Mon	
Tue	
Wed	
Thu	
Fri	
Sat	
Sun	

Monday | 8 June 2026 - Last Quarter

6:00	Today's quick wins	
7:00		
8:00		
9:00		
10:00		
11:00	Health and nutrition	
12:00		
13:00		
14:00	Today, I am grateful for...	
15:00		
16:00		
17:00	Today's self care	
18:00		
19:00		
20:00	Chart your cycle	
21:00		
22:00		
23:00	Positive affirmation	
Notes		

Tuesday | 9 June 2026 - Waning Crescent

6:00		Today's quick wins
7:00		
8:00		
9:00		
10:00		
11:00		Health and nutrition
12:00		
13:00		
14:00		Today, I am grateful for...
15:00		
16:00		
17:00		Today's self care
18:00		
19:00		
20:00		Chart your cycle
21:00		
22:00		
23:00		Positive affirmation
Notes		

Wednesday | 10 June 2026 - Waning Crescent

6:00	**Today's quick wins**
7:00	
8:00	
9:00	
10:00	
11:00	**Health and nutrition**
12:00	
13:00	
14:00	**Today, I am grateful for...**
15:00	
16:00	
17:00	**Today's self care**
18:00	
19:00	
20:00	**Chart your cycle**
21:00	
22:00	
23:00	**Positive affirmation**
Notes	

Thursday | 11 June 2026 - Waning Crescent

6:00	**Today's quick wins**
7:00	
8:00	
9:00	
10:00	
11:00	**Health and nutrition**
12:00	
13:00	
14:00	**Today, I am grateful for...**
15:00	
16:00	
17:00	**Today's self care**
18:00	
19:00	
20:00	**Chart your cycle**
21:00	
22:00	
23:00	**Positive affirmation**
Notes	

Friday | 12 June 2026 - Waning Crescent

6:00	**Today's quick wins**
7:00	
8:00	
9:00	
10:00	
11:00	**Health and nutrition**
12:00	
13:00	
14:00	**Today, I am grateful for...**
15:00	
16:00	
17:00	**Today's self care**
18:00	
19:00	
20:00	**Chart your cycle**
21:00	
22:00	
23:00	**Positive affirmation**
Notes	

Saturday | 13 June 2026 - Waning Crescent

6:00	**Today's quick wins**
7:00	
8:00	
9:00	
10:00	
11:00	**Health and nutrition**
12:00	
13:00	
14:00	**Today, I am grateful for...**
15:00	
16:00	
17:00	**Today's self care**
18:00	
19:00	
20:00	**Chart your cycle**
21:00	
22:00	
23:00	**Positive affirmation**
Notes	

Sunday | 14 June 2026 - Waning Crescent

6:00	**Today's quick wins**
7:00	
8:00	
9:00	
10:00	
11:00	**Health and nutrition**
12:00	
13:00	
14:00	**Today, I am grateful for...**
15:00	
16:00	
17:00	**Today's self care**
18:00	
19:00	
20:00	**Chart your cycle**
21:00	
22:00	
23:00	**Positive affirmation**
Notes	

My Week 15th Jun - 21st Jun

Day	
Mon	
Tue	
Wed	
Thu	
Fri	
Sat	
Sun	

Monday | 15 June 2026 - New Moon in Gemini at 02.53 GMT

6:00	Today's quick wins
7:00	
8:00	
9:00	
10:00	
11:00	Health and nutrition
12:00	
13:00	
14:00	Today, I am grateful for...
15:00	
16:00	
17:00	Today's self care
18:00	
19:00	
20:00	Chart your cycle
21:00	
22:00	
23:00	Positive affirmation
Notes	

Tuesday | 16 June 2026 - Waxing Crescent

6:00		Today's quick wins
7:00		
8:00		
9:00		
10:00		
11:00		Health and nutrition
12:00		
13:00		
14:00		Today, I am grateful for...
15:00		
16:00		
17:00		Today's self care
18:00		
19:00		
20:00		Chart your cycle
21:00		
22:00		
23:00		Positive affirmation
Notes		

Wednesday | 17 June 2026 - Waxing Crescent

6:00	Today's quick wins	
7:00		
8:00		
9:00		
10:00		
11:00	Health and nutrition	
12:00		
13:00		
14:00	Today, I am grateful for...	
15:00		
16:00		
17:00	Today's self care	
18:00		
19:00		
20:00	Chart your cycle	
21:00		
22:00		
23:00	Positive affirmation	
Notes		

Thursday | 18 June 2026 - Waxing Crescent

6:00		Today's quick wins
7:00		
8:00		
9:00		
10:00		
11:00		Health and nutrition
12:00		
13:00		
14:00		Today, I am grateful for...
15:00		
16:00		
17:00		Today's self care
18:00		
19:00		
20:00		Chart your cycle
21:00		
22:00		
23:00		Positive affirmation
Notes		

Friday | 19 June 2026 - Waxing Crescent

6:00	Today's quick wins
7:00	
8:00	
9:00	
10:00	
11:00	Health and nutrition
12:00	
13:00	
14:00	Today, I am grateful for...
15:00	
16:00	
17:00	Today's self care
18:00	
19:00	
20:00	Chart your cycle
21:00	
22:00	
23:00	Positive affirmation
Notes	

Saturday	20 June 2026 - Waxing Crescent
6:00	Today's quick wins
7:00	
8:00	
9:00	
10:00	
11:00	Health and nutrition
12:00	
13:00	
14:00	Today, I am grateful for...
15:00	
16:00	
17:00	Today's self care
18:00	
19:00	
20:00	Chart your cycle
21:00	
22:00	
23:00	Positive affirmation
Notes	

Sunday | 21 June 2026 - First Quarter - *Summer Solstice*

6:00	**Today's quick wins**
7:00	
8:00	
9:00	
10:00	
11:00	**Health and nutrition**
12:00	
13:00	
14:00	**Today, I am grateful for...**
15:00	
16:00	
17:00	**Today's self care**
18:00	
19:00	
20:00	**Chart your cycle**
21:00	
22:00	
23:00	**Positive affirmation**
Notes	

My Week 22nd Jun – 28th Jun

Day	
Mon	
Tue	
Wed	
Thu	
Fri	
Sat	
Sun	

Monday | 22 June 2026 - First Quarter

6:00	Today's quick wins	
7:00		
8:00		
9:00		
10:00		
11:00	Health and nutrition	
12:00		
13:00		
14:00	Today, I am grateful for...	
15:00		
16:00		
17:00	Today's self care	
18:00		
19:00		
20:00	Chart your cycle	
21:00		
22:00		
23:00	Positive affirmation	
Notes		

Tuesday | 23 June 2026 - Waxing Gibbous

6:00		Today's quick wins
7:00		
8:00		
9:00		
10:00		
11:00		Health and nutrition
12:00		
13:00		
14:00		Today, I am grateful for...
15:00		
16:00		
17:00		Today's self care
18:00		
19:00		
20:00		Chart your cycle
21:00		
22:00		
23:00		Positive affirmation
Notes		

Wednesday | 24 June 2026 - Waxing Gibbous

6:00		Today's quick wins
7:00		
8:00		
9:00		
10:00		
11:00		Health and nutrition
12:00		
13:00		
14:00		Today, I am grateful for...
15:00		
16:00		
17:00		Today's self care
18:00		
19:00		
20:00		Chart your cycle
21:00		
22:00		
23:00		Positive affirmation
Notes		

Thursday | 25 June 2026 - Waxing Gibbous

6:00		Today's quick wins	
7:00			
8:00			
9:00			
10:00			
11:00		Health and nutrition	
12:00			
13:00			
14:00		Today, I am grateful for...	
15:00			
16:00			
17:00		Today's self care	
18:00			
19:00			
20:00		Chart your cycle	
21:00			
22:00			
23:00		Positive affirmation	
Notes			

Friday | 26 June 2026 - Waxing Gibbous

6:00		Today's quick wins
7:00		
8:00		
9:00		
10:00		
11:00		Health and nutrition
12:00		
13:00		
14:00		Today, I am grateful for...
15:00		
16:00		
17:00		Today's self care
18:00		
19:00		
20:00		Chart your cycle
21:00		
22:00		
23:00		Positive affirmation
Notes		

Saturday | 27 June 2026 - Waxing Gibbous

6:00		Today's quick wins	
7:00			
8:00			
9:00			
10:00			
11:00		Health and nutrition	
12:00			
13:00			
14:00		Today, I am grateful for…	
15:00			
16:00			
17:00		Today's self care	
18:00			
19:00			
20:00		Chart your cycle	
21:00			
22:00			
23:00		Positive affirmation	
Notes			

Sunday | 28 June 2026 - Waxing Gibbous

6:00	**Today's quick wins**
7:00	
8:00	
9:00	
10:00	
11:00	**Health and nutrition**
12:00	
13:00	
14:00	**Today, I am grateful for...**
15:00	
16:00	
17:00	**Today's self care**
18:00	
19:00	
20:00	**Chart your cycle**
21:00	
22:00	
23:00	**Positive affirmation**
Notes	

My Week 29th Jun - 5th Jul

Mon	
Tue	
Wed	
Thu	
Fri	
Sat	
Sun	

Monday | 29 June 2026 - Full Moon in Capricorn at 23.56 GMT

6:00	Today's quick wins
7:00	
8:00	
9:00	
10:00	
11:00	Health and nutrition
12:00	
13:00	
14:00	Today, I am grateful for...
15:00	
16:00	
17:00	Today's self care
18:00	
19:00	
20:00	Chart your cycle
21:00	
22:00	
23:00	Positive affirmation
Notes	

Tuesday | 30 June 2026 - Waning Gibbous

6:00		Today's quick wins
7:00		
8:00		
9:00		
10:00		
11:00		Health and nutrition
12:00		
13:00		
14:00		Today, I am grateful for...
15:00		
16:00		
17:00		Today's self care
18:00		
19:00		
20:00		Chart your cycle
21:00		
22:00		
23:00		Positive affirmation
Notes		

June achievements

Be proud of yourself and all that you have achieved this month. Write down your wins, big and small. If you have not achieved everything that you set out to do, that's okay! We learn and grow through our mistakes and experiences. You can use this space to make notes about anything that you have learned.

July 2026

Notes	Monday	Tuesday	Wednesday
	29	30	1
	6	7	8
	13	14	15
	20	21	22
	27	28	29

Thursday	Friday	Saturday	Sunday
2	3	4	5
9	10	11	12
16	17	18	19
23	24	25	26
30	31	1	2

July
Goddess Pele

PELE

Pele is not a calm ocean or gentle breeze. She's more lava in a red dress that both creates and consumes. Born of raw earth, old blood, and a heat that reshapes the map.

She came from far across the sea, from the sacred lands of Kahiki. Legend says she travelled in a canoe and every step she took carved the bones of Hawaii.

She doesn't take disrespect. Not from mortals or from gods. Not from anyone who forgets that creation always comes with risk.
Without her, there's no soil, no new birth, no fresh breath for the next world. Pele doesn't destroy to punish, but to purify and begin again.

She's fierce, but also beautiful and her moods are unpredictable. Her heart has a molten core that can level cities, or cradle you in light.

People leave her offerings of flowers, rum, hair and tears.
Pele doesn't wait for permission.
She doesn't ask for worship.
She is the altar.

Crystal: Create a volcanic altar with lava stone, obsidian, and red flowers

My Vision for July

Wednesday | 1 July 2026 - Waning Gibbous

6:00		Today's quick wins	
7:00			
8:00			
9:00			
10:00			
11:00		Health and nutrition	
12:00			
13:00			
14:00		Today, I am grateful for...	
15:00			
16:00			
17:00		Today's self care	
18:00			
19:00			
20:00		Chart your cycle	
21:00			
22:00			
23:00		Positive affirmation	
Notes			

Thursday | 2 July 2026 - Waning Gibbous

6:00	**Today's quick wins**
7:00	
8:00	
9:00	
10:00	
11:00	**Health and nutrition**
12:00	
13:00	
14:00	**Today, I am grateful for...**
15:00	
16:00	
17:00	**Today's self care**
18:00	
19:00	
20:00	**Chart your cycle**
21:00	
22:00	
23:00	**Positive affirmation**
Notes	

Friday | 3 July 2026 - Waning Gibbous

6:00		Today's quick wins
7:00		
8:00		
9:00		
10:00		
11:00		Health and nutrition
12:00		
13:00		
14:00		Today, I am grateful for...
15:00		
16:00		
17:00		Today's self care
18:00		
19:00		
20:00		Chart your cycle
21:00		
22:00		
23:00		Positive affirmation
Notes		

Saturday | 4 July 2026 - Waning Gibbous

6:00	**Today's quick wins**
7:00	
8:00	
9:00	
10:00	
11:00	**Health and nutrition**
12:00	
13:00	
14:00	**Today, I am grateful for...**
15:00	
16:00	
17:00	**Today's self care**
18:00	
19:00	
20:00	**Chart your cycle**
21:00	
22:00	
23:00	**Positive affirmation**
Notes	

Sunday | 5 July 2026 - Waning Gibbous

6:00		Today's quick wins
7:00		
8:00		
9:00		
10:00		
11:00		Health and nutrition
12:00		
13:00		
14:00		Today, I am grateful for...
15:00		
16:00		
17:00		Today's self care
18:00		
19:00		
20:00		Chart your cycle
21:00		
22:00		
23:00		Positive affirmation
Notes		

My Week 6th Jul - 12th Jul

Mon	
Tue	
Wed	
Thu	
Fri	
Sat	
Sun	

Monday | 6 July 2026 - Waning Gibbous

6:00	Today's quick wins
7:00	
8:00	
9:00	
10:00	
11:00	Health and nutrition
12:00	
13:00	
14:00	Today, I am grateful for...
15:00	
16:00	
17:00	Today's self care
18:00	
19:00	
20:00	Chart your cycle
21:00	
22:00	
23:00	Positive affirmation
Notes	

Tuesday | 7 July 2026 - Last Quarter

6:00	Today's quick wins
7:00	
8:00	
9:00	
10:00	
11:00	Health and nutrition
12:00	
13:00	
14:00	Today, I am grateful for...
15:00	
16:00	
17:00	Today's self care
18:00	
19:00	
20:00	Chart your cycle
21:00	
22:00	
23:00	Positive affirmation
Notes	

Wednesday | 8 July 2026 - Waning Crescent

6:00	**Today's quick wins**
7:00	
8:00	
9:00	
10:00	
11:00	**Health and nutrition**
12:00	
13:00	
14:00	**Today, I am grateful for...**
15:00	
16:00	
17:00	**Today's self care**
18:00	
19:00	
20:00	**Chart your cycle**
21:00	
22:00	
23:00	**Positive affirmation**
Notes	

Thursday | 9 July 2026 - Waning Crescent

6:00	**Today's quick wins**	
7:00		
8:00		
9:00		
10:00		
11:00	**Health and nutrition**	
12:00		
13:00		
14:00	**Today, I am grateful for...**	
15:00		
16:00		
17:00	**Today's self care**	
18:00		
19:00		
20:00	**Chart your cycle**	
21:00		
22:00		
23:00	**Positive affirmation**	
Notes		

Friday | 10 July 2026 - Waning Crescent

6:00	**Today's quick wins**
7:00	
8:00	
9:00	
10:00	
11:00	**Health and nutrition**
12:00	
13:00	
14:00	**Today, I am grateful for...**
15:00	
16:00	
17:00	**Today's self care**
18:00	
19:00	
20:00	**Chart your cycle**
21:00	
22:00	
23:00	**Positive affirmation**
Notes	

Saturday | 11 July 2026 - Waning Crescent

6:00	**Today's quick wins**
7:00	
8:00	
9:00	
10:00	
11:00	**Health and nutrition**
12:00	
13:00	
14:00	**Today, I am grateful for...**
15:00	
16:00	
17:00	**Today's self care**
18:00	
19:00	
20:00	**Chart your cycle**
21:00	
22:00	
23:00	**Positive affirmation**
Notes	

Sunday | 12 July 2026 - Waning Crescent

6:00		Today's quick wins
7:00		
8:00		
9:00		
10:00		
11:00		Health and nutrition
12:00		
13:00		
14:00		Today, I am grateful for...
15:00		
16:00		
17:00		Today's self care
18:00		
19:00		
20:00		Chart your cycle
21:00		
22:00		
23:00		Positive affirmation
Notes		

My Week 13th Jul - 19th Jul

Mon	
Tue	
Wed	
Thu	
Fri	
Sat	
Sun	

Monday | 13 July 2026 - Waning Crescent

6:00		Today's quick wins
7:00		
8:00		
9:00		
10:00		
11:00		Health and nutrition
12:00		
13:00		
14:00		Today, I am grateful for...
15:00		
16:00		
17:00		Today's self care
18:00		
19:00		
20:00		Chart your cycle
21:00		
22:00		
23:00		Positive affirmation
Notes		

Tuesday | 14 July 2026 - New Moon in Cancer at 09.43 GMT

6:00	Today's quick wins	
7:00		
8:00		
9:00		
10:00		
11:00	Health and nutrition	
12:00		
13:00		
14:00	Today, I am grateful for...	
15:00		
16:00		
17:00	Today's self care	
18:00		
19:00		
20:00	Chart your cycle	
21:00		
22:00		
23:00	Positive affirmation	
Notes		

Wednesday | 15 July 2026 - Waxing Crescent

6:00	**Today's quick wins**
7:00	
8:00	
9:00	
10:00	
11:00	**Health and nutrition**
12:00	
13:00	
14:00	**Today, I am grateful for...**
15:00	
16:00	
17:00	**Today's self care**
18:00	
19:00	
20:00	**Chart your cycle**
21:00	
22:00	
23:00	**Positive affirmation**

Notes

Thursday | 16 July 2026 - Waxing Crescent

6:00	Today's quick wins	
7:00		
8:00		
9:00		
10:00		
11:00	Health and nutrition	
12:00		
13:00		
14:00	Today, I am grateful for...	
15:00		
16:00		
17:00	Today's self care	
18:00		
19:00		
20:00	Chart your cycle	
21:00		
22:00		
23:00	Positive affirmation	
Notes		

Friday | 17 July 2026 - Waxing Crescent

6:00		Today's quick wins	
7:00			
8:00			
9:00			
10:00			
11:00		Health and nutrition	
12:00			
13:00			
14:00		Today, I am grateful for...	
15:00			
16:00			
17:00		Today's self care	
18:00			
19:00			
20:00		Chart your cycle	
21:00			
22:00			
23:00		Positive affirmation	
Notes			

Saturday | 18 July 2026 - Waxing Crescent

6:00	Today's quick wins	
7:00		
8:00		
9:00		
10:00		
11:00	Health and nutrition	
12:00		
13:00		
14:00	Today, I am grateful for…	
15:00		
16:00		
17:00	Today's self care	
18:00		
19:00		
20:00	Chart your cycle	
21:00		
22:00		
23:00	Positive affirmation	
Notes		

Sunday | 19 July 2026 - Waxing Crescent

6:00	Today's quick wins
7:00	
8:00	
9:00	
10:00	
11:00	Health and nutrition
12:00	
13:00	
14:00	Today, I am grateful for...
15:00	
16:00	
17:00	Today's self care
18:00	
19:00	
20:00	Chart your cycle
21:00	
22:00	
23:00	Positive affirmation
Notes	

My Week 20th Jul - 26th Jul

Mon	
Tue	
Wed	
Thu	
Fri	
Sat	
Sun	

Monday | 20 July 2026 - Waxing Crescent

6:00	Today's quick wins	
7:00		
8:00		
9:00		
10:00		
11:00	Health and nutrition	
12:00		
13:00		
14:00	Today, I am grateful for...	
15:00		
16:00		
17:00	Today's self care	
18:00		
19:00		
20:00	Chart your cycle	
21:00		
22:00		
23:00	Positive affirmation	
Notes		

Tuesday | 21 July 2026 - First Quarter

6:00	Today's quick wins	
7:00		
8:00		
9:00		
10:00		
11:00	Health and nutrition	
12:00		
13:00		
14:00	Today, I am grateful for...	
15:00		
16:00		
17:00	Today's self care	
18:00		
19:00		
20:00	Chart your cycle	
21:00		
22:00		
23:00	Positive affirmation	
Notes		

Wednesday | 22 July 2026 - Waxing Gibbous

6:00		Today's quick wins	
7:00			
8:00			
9:00			
10:00			
11:00		Health and nutrition	
12:00			
13:00			
14:00		Today, I am grateful for...	
15:00			
16:00			
17:00		Today's self care	
18:00			
19:00			
20:00		Chart your cycle	
21:00			
22:00			
23:00		Positive affirmation	
Notes			

Thursday | 23 July 2026 - Waxing Gibbous

6:00	Today's quick wins
7:00	
8:00	
9:00	
10:00	
11:00	Health and nutrition
12:00	
13:00	
14:00	Today, I am grateful for...
15:00	
16:00	
17:00	Today's self care
18:00	
19:00	
20:00	Chart your cycle
21:00	
22:00	
23:00	Positive affirmation
Notes	

Friday | 24 July 2026 - Waxing Gibbous

6:00	**Today's quick wins**
7:00	
8:00	
9:00	
10:00	
11:00	**Health and nutrition**
12:00	
13:00	
14:00	**Today, I am grateful for...**
15:00	
16:00	
17:00	**Today's self care**
18:00	
19:00	
20:00	**Chart your cycle**
21:00	
22:00	
23:00	**Positive affirmation** |//
Notes	

Saturday | 25 July 2026 - Waxing Gibbous

6:00	**Today's quick wins**	
7:00		
8:00		
9:00		
10:00		
11:00	**Health and nutrition**	
12:00		
13:00		
14:00	**Today, I am grateful for...**	
15:00		
16:00		
17:00	**Today's self care**	
18:00		
19:00		
20:00	**Chart your cycle**	
21:00		
22:00		
23:00	**Positive affirmation**	
Notes		

Sunday | 26 July 2026 - Waxing Gibbous

6:00	Today's quick wins	
7:00		
8:00		
9:00		
10:00		
11:00	Health and nutrition	
12:00		
13:00		
14:00	Today, I am grateful for...	
15:00		
16:00		
17:00	Today's self care	
18:00		
19:00		
20:00	Chart your cycle	
21:00		
22:00		
23:00	Positive affirmation	
Notes		

My Week 27th Jul - 2nd Aug

Mon	
Tue	
Wed	
Thu	
Fri	
Sat	
Sun	

Monday | 27 July 2026 - Waxing Gibbous

6:00		Today's quick wins	
7:00			
8:00			
9:00			
10:00			
11:00		Health and nutrition	
12:00			
13:00			
14:00		Today, I am grateful for...	
15:00			
16:00			
17:00		Today's self care	
18:00			
19:00			
20:00		Chart your cycle	
21:00			
22:00			
23:00		Positive affirmation	
Notes			

Tuesday | 28 July 2026 - Waxing Gibbous

6:00	Today's quick wins
7:00	
8:00	
9:00	
10:00	
11:00	Health and nutrition
12:00	
13:00	
14:00	Today, I am grateful for...
15:00	
16:00	
17:00	Today's self care
18:00	
19:00	
20:00	Chart your cycle
21:00	
22:00	
23:00	Positive affirmation
Notes	

Wednesday | 29 July 2026 - Full Moon in Aquarius at 14.35GMT

6:00	**Today's quick wins**
7:00	
8:00	
9:00	
10:00	
11:00	**Health and nutrition**
12:00	
13:00	
14:00	**Today, I am grateful for...**
15:00	
16:00	
17:00	**Today's self care**
18:00	
19:00	
20:00	**Chart your cycle**
21:00	
22:00	
23:00	**Positive affirmation**
Notes	

Thursday | 30 July 2026 - Waning Gibbous

6:00	Today's quick wins	
7:00		
8:00		
9:00		
10:00		
11:00	Health and nutrition	
12:00		
13:00		
14:00	Today, I am grateful for...	
15:00		
16:00		
17:00	Today's self care	
18:00		
19:00		
20:00	Chart your cycle	
21:00		
22:00		
23:00	Positive affirmation	
Notes		

Friday	31 July 2026 - Waning Gibbous
6:00	Today's quick wins
7:00	
8:00	
9:00	
10:00	
11:00	Health and nutrition
12:00	
13:00	
14:00	Today, I am grateful for...
15:00	
16:00	
17:00	Today's self care
18:00	
19:00	
20:00	Chart your cycle
21:00	
22:00	
23:00	Positive affirmation
Notes	

July achievements

Be proud of yourself and all that you have achieved this month. Write down your wins, big and small. If you have not achieved everything that you set out to do, that's okay! We learn and grow through our mistakes and experiences. You can use this space to make notes about anything that you have learned.

August 2026

Notes	Monday	Tuesday	Wednesday
	27	28	29
	3	4	5
	10	11	12 *Solar Eclipse* ●
	17	18	19
	24 / 31	25	26

Thursday	Friday	Saturday	Sunday
30	31	1	2
6 ☽	7	8	9
13	14	15	16
20 ☾	21	22	23
27	28 ○ Lunar Eclipse	29	30

August
Goddess Oshun

OSHUN

Oshun arrives drenched in gold with her hips moving like prayer. She is the Orisha of fresh water, love, beauty, fertility and sensuality.

They say when the world was dry and brittle, when her wisdom was ignored and the earth started dying, Oshun withdrew. There was no laughter or love. Everything began to crumble. That's when they remembered that nothing moves without her. Not love. Not life. Not light.

You don't demand from her. You honour her. You show up with offerings such as honey, oranges, cinnamon, mirrors-because she reflects what you bring. You bring love, she gives you more. You bring lies, she'll drown you in the truth.

And don't underestimate her just because she smiles. Oshun can heal with a kiss or hex with a glance. She is the river: calm until she's not. Smooth until she rises. Ask the ones who disrespected her. Ask the kings who thought they didn't need her. She left them thirsty.

Oshun is for those who know that softness is not weakness.
She is a mirror,
and in her waters, you will meet yourself.

Crystal: Yellow Agate - use for higher awareness of your inner self. Light a gold or yellow candle, and offer her cinnamon, honey, or oranges.

My Vision for August

Saturday | 1 August 2026 - Waning Gibbous

6:00	**Today's quick wins**
7:00	
8:00	
9:00	
10:00	
11:00	**Health and nutrition**
12:00	
13:00	
14:00	**Today, I am grateful for...**
15:00	
16:00	
17:00	**Today's self care**
18:00	
19:00	
20:00	**Chart your cycle**
21:00	
22:00	
23:00	**Positive affirmation**
Notes	

Sunday | 2 August 2026 - Waning Gibbous

6:00	**Today's quick wins**
7:00	
8:00	
9:00	
10:00	
11:00	**Health and nutrition**
12:00	
13:00	
14:00	**Today, I am grateful for...**
15:00	
16:00	
17:00	**Today's self care**
18:00	
19:00	
20:00	**Chart your cycle**
21:00	
22:00	
23:00	**Positive affirmation**
Notes	

My Week 3rd Aug - 9th Aug

Mon	
Tue	
Wed	
Thu	
Fri	
Sat	
Sun	

Monday | 3 August 2026 - Waning Gibbous

6:00	Today's quick wins
7:00	
8:00	
9:00	
10:00	
11:00	Health and nutrition
12:00	
13:00	
14:00	Today, I am grateful for...
15:00	
16:00	
17:00	Today's self care
18:00	
19:00	
20:00	Chart your cycle
21:00	
22:00	
23:00	Positive affirmation
Notes	

Tuesday | 4 August 2026 - Waning Gibbous

6:00	Today's quick wins
7:00	
8:00	
9:00	
10:00	
11:00	Health and nutrition
12:00	
13:00	
14:00	Today, I am grateful for...
15:00	
16:00	
17:00	Today's self care
18:00	
19:00	
20:00	Chart your cycle
21:00	
22:00	
23:00	Positive affirmation
Notes	

Wednesday | 5 August 2026 - Waning Gibbous

6:00		**Today's quick wins**	
7:00			
8:00			
9:00			
10:00			
11:00		**Health and nutrition**	
12:00			
13:00			
14:00		**Today, I am grateful for…**	
15:00			
16:00			
17:00		**Today's self care**	
18:00			
19:00			
20:00		**Chart your cycle**	
21:00			
22:00			
23:00		**Positive affirmation**	
Notes			

Thursday | 6 August 2026 - Last Quarter

6:00	**Today's quick wins**
7:00	
8:00	
9:00	
10:00	
11:00	**Health and nutrition**
12:00	
13:00	
14:00	**Today, I am grateful for...**
15:00	
16:00	
17:00	**Today's self care**
18:00	
19:00	
20:00	**Chart your cycle**
21:00	
22:00	
23:00	**Positive affirmation**
Notes	

Friday | 7 August 2026 - Waning Crescent

6:00	**Today's quick wins**
7:00	
8:00	
9:00	
10:00	
11:00	**Health and nutrition**
12:00	
13:00	
14:00	**Today, I am grateful for...**
15:00	
16:00	
17:00	**Today's self care**
18:00	
19:00	
20:00	**Chart your cycle**
21:00	
22:00	
23:00	**Positive affirmation**
Notes	

Saturday | 8 August 2026 - Waning Crescent

6:00	Today's quick wins	
7:00		
8:00		
9:00		
10:00		
11:00	Health and nutrition	
12:00		
13:00		
14:00	Today, I am grateful for…	
15:00		
16:00		
17:00	Today's self care	
18:00		
19:00		
20:00	Chart your cycle	
21:00		
22:00		
23:00	Positive affirmation	
Notes		

Sunday | 9 August 2026 - Waning Crescent

6:00		Today's quick wins
7:00		
8:00		
9:00		
10:00		
11:00		Health and nutrition
12:00		
13:00		
14:00		Today, I am grateful for...
15:00		
16:00		
17:00		Today's self care
18:00		
19:00		
20:00		Chart your cycle
21:00		
22:00		
23:00		Positive affirmation
Notes		

My Week 10th Aug – 16th Aug

Mon	
Tue	
Wed	
Thu	
Fri	
Sat	
Sun	

Monday | 10 August 2026 - Waning Crescent

6:00		Today's quick wins
7:00		
8:00		
9:00		
10:00		
11:00		Health and nutrition
12:00		
13:00		
14:00		Today, I am grateful for...
15:00		
16:00		
17:00		Today's self care
18:00		
19:00		
20:00		Chart your cycle
21:00		
22:00		
23:00		Positive affirmation
Notes		

Tuesday | 11 August 2026 - Waning Crescent

6:00		Today's quick wins	
7:00			
8:00			
9:00			
10:00			
11:00		Health and nutrition	
12:00			
13:00			
14:00		Today, I am grateful for...	
15:00			
16:00			
17:00		Today's self care	
18:00			
19:00			
20:00		Chart your cycle	
21:00			
22:00			
23:00		Positive affirmation	
Notes			

Wednesday | 12 August 2026 - New Moon Solar Eclipse in Leo at 17.36 GMT

6:00		Today's quick wins
7:00		
8:00		
9:00		
10:00		
11:00		Health and nutrition
12:00		
13:00		
14:00		Today, I am grateful for...
15:00		
16:00		
17:00		Today's self care
18:00		
19:00		
20:00		Chart your cycle
21:00		
22:00		
23:00		Positive affirmation
Notes		

Thursday | 13 August 2026 - Waxing Crescent

6:00	**Today's quick wins**
7:00	
8:00	
9:00	
10:00	
11:00	**Health and nutrition**
12:00	
13:00	
14:00	**Today, I am grateful for...**
15:00	
16:00	
17:00	**Today's self care**
18:00	
19:00	
20:00	**Chart your cycle**
21:00	
22:00	
23:00	**Positive affirmation**
Notes	

Friday | 14 August 2026 - Waxing Crescent

6:00	**Today's quick wins**
7:00	
8:00	
9:00	
10:00	
11:00	**Health and nutrition**
12:00	
13:00	
14:00	**Today, I am grateful for...**
15:00	
16:00	
17:00	**Today's self care**
18:00	
19:00	
20:00	**Chart your cycle**
21:00	
22:00	
23:00	**Positive affirmation**
Notes	

Saturday | 15 August 2026 - Waxing Crescent

6:00	**Today's quick wins**
7:00	
8:00	
9:00	
10:00	
11:00	**Health and nutrition**
12:00	
13:00	
14:00	**Today, I am grateful for...**
15:00	
16:00	
17:00	**Today's self care**
18:00	
19:00	
20:00	**Chart your cycle**
21:00	
22:00	
23:00	**Positive affirmation**
Notes	

Sunday | 16 August 2026 - Waxing Crescent

6:00	Today's quick wins	
7:00		
8:00		
9:00		
10:00		
11:00	Health and nutrition	
12:00		
13:00		
14:00	Today, I am grateful for...	
15:00		
16:00		
17:00	Today's self care	
18:00		
19:00		
20:00	Chart your cycle	
21:00		
22:00		
23:00	Positive affirmation	
Notes		

My Week 17th Aug - 23rd Aug

Day	
Mon	
Tue	
Wed	
Thu	
Fri	
Sat	
Sun	

Monday | 17 August 2026 - Waxing Crescent

6:00	**Today's quick wins**
7:00	
8:00	
9:00	
10:00	
11:00	**Health and nutrition**
12:00	
13:00	
14:00	**Today, I am grateful for...**
15:00	
16:00	
17:00	**Today's self care**
18:00	
19:00	
20:00	**Chart your cycle**
21:00	
22:00	
23:00	**Positive affirmation**
Notes	

Tuesday | 18 August 2026 - Waxing Crescent

6:00		Today's quick wins	
7:00			
8:00			
9:00			
10:00			
11:00		Health and nutrition	
12:00			
13:00			
14:00		Today, I am grateful for...	
15:00			
16:00			
17:00		Today's self care	
18:00			
19:00			
20:00		Chart your cycle	
21:00			
22:00			
23:00		Positive affirmation	
Notes			

Wednesday | 19 August 2026 - First Quarter

6:00	Today's quick wins
7:00	
8:00	
9:00	
10:00	
11:00	Health and nutrition
12:00	
13:00	
14:00	Today, I am grateful for...
15:00	
16:00	
17:00	Today's self care
18:00	
19:00	
20:00	Chart your cycle
21:00	
22:00	
23:00	Positive affirmation
Notes	

Thursday | 20 August 2026 - First Quarter

6:00	**Today's quick wins**
7:00	
8:00	
9:00	
10:00	
11:00	**Health and nutrition**
12:00	
13:00	
14:00	**Today, I am grateful for...**
15:00	
16:00	
17:00	**Today's self care**
18:00	
19:00	
20:00	**Chart your cycle**
21:00	
22:00	
23:00	**Positive affirmation**
Notes	

Friday | 21 August 2026 - Waxing Gibbous

6:00	Today's quick wins
7:00	
8:00	
9:00	
10:00	
11:00	Health and nutrition
12:00	
13:00	
14:00	Today, I am grateful for...
15:00	
16:00	
17:00	Today's self care
18:00	
19:00	
20:00	Chart your cycle
21:00	
22:00	
23:00	Positive affirmation
Notes	

Saturday | 22 August 2026 - Waxing Gibbous

6:00	**Today's quick wins**
7:00	
8:00	
9:00	
10:00	
11:00	**Health and nutrition**
12:00	
13:00	
14:00	**Today, I am grateful for...**
15:00	
16:00	
17:00	**Today's self care**
18:00	
19:00	
20:00	**Chart your cycle**
21:00	
22:00	
23:00	**Positive affirmation**
Notes	

Sunday | 23 August 2026 - Waxing Gibbous

6:00	Today's quick wins	
7:00		
8:00		
9:00		
10:00		
11:00	Health and nutrition	
12:00		
13:00		
14:00	Today, I am grateful for...	
15:00		
16:00		
17:00	Today's self care	
18:00		
19:00		
20:00	Chart your cycle	
21:00		
22:00		
23:00	Positive affirmation	
Notes		

My Week 24th Aug - 30th Aug

Mon	
Tue	
Wed	
Thu	
Fri	
Sat	
Sun	

Monday | 24 August 2026 - Waxing Gibbous

6:00	**Today's quick wins**
7:00	
8:00	
9:00	
10:00	
11:00	**Health and nutrition**
12:00	
13:00	
14:00	**Today, I am grateful for...**
15:00	
16:00	
17:00	**Today's self care**
18:00	
19:00	
20:00	**Chart your cycle**
21:00	
22:00	
23:00	**Positive affirmation**
Notes	

Tuesday | 25 August 2026 - Waxing Gibbous

6:00	**Today's quick wins**
7:00	
8:00	
9:00	
10:00	
11:00	**Health and nutrition**
12:00	
13:00	
14:00	**Today, I am grateful for...**
15:00	
16:00	
17:00	**Today's self care**
18:00	
19:00	
20:00	**Chart your cycle**
21:00	
22:00	
23:00	**Positive affirmation**
Notes	

Wednesday | 26 August 2026 - Waxing Gibbous

6:00	Today's quick wins	
7:00		
8:00		
9:00		
10:00		
11:00	Health and nutrition	
12:00		
13:00		
14:00	Today, I am grateful for...	
15:00		
16:00		
17:00	Today's self care	
18:00		
19:00		
20:00	Chart your cycle	
21:00		
22:00		
23:00	Positive affirmation	
Notes		

Thursday | 27 August 2026 - Waxing Gibbous

6:00		Today's quick wins
7:00		
8:00		
9:00		
10:00		
11:00		Health and nutrition
12:00		
13:00		
14:00		Today, I am grateful for...
15:00		
16:00		
17:00		Today's self care
18:00		
19:00		
20:00		Chart your cycle
21:00		
22:00		
23:00		Positive affirmation
Notes		

Friday | 28 August 2026 - Full Moon Lunar Eclipse in Pisces at 04.18 GMT

6:00	**Today's quick wins**
7:00	
8:00	
9:00	
10:00	
11:00	**Health and nutrition**
12:00	
13:00	
14:00	**Today, I am grateful for...**
15:00	
16:00	
17:00	**Today's self care**
18:00	
19:00	
20:00	**Chart your cycle**
21:00	
22:00	
23:00	**Positive affirmation**
Notes	

Saturday | 29 August 2026 - Waning Gibbous

6:00	**Today's quick wins**
7:00	
8:00	
9:00	
10:00	
11:00	**Health and nutrition**
12:00	
13:00	
14:00	**Today, I am grateful for...**
15:00	
16:00	
17:00	**Today's self care**
18:00	
19:00	
20:00	**Chart your cycle**
21:00	
22:00	
23:00	**Positive affirmation**

Notes

Sunday | 30 August 2026 - Waning Gibbous

6:00	**Today's quick wins**
7:00	
8:00	
9:00	
10:00	
11:00	**Health and nutrition**
12:00	
13:00	
14:00	**Today, I am grateful for...**
15:00	
16:00	
17:00	**Today's self care**
18:00	
19:00	
20:00	**Chart your cycle**
21:00	
22:00	
23:00	**Positive affirmation**
Notes	

My Week 31st Aug - 6th Sep

Mon	
Tue	
Wed	
Thu	
Fri	
Sat	
Sun	

Monday | 31 August 2026 - Waning Gibbous

6:00	**Today's quick wins**
7:00	
8:00	
9:00	
10:00	
11:00	**Health and nutrition**
12:00	
13:00	
14:00	**Today, I am grateful for...**
15:00	
16:00	
17:00	**Today's self care**
18:00	
19:00	
20:00	**Chart your cycle**
21:00	
22:00	
23:00	**Positive affirmation**
Notes	

August achievements

Be proud of yourself and all that you have achieved this month. Write down your wins, big and small. If you have not achieved everything that you set out to do, that's okay! We learn and grow through our mistakes and experiences. You can use this space to make notes about anything that you have learned.

'In Haudenoshonee society, leaders are encouraged to remember seven generations in the past and consider seven generations in the future when making decisions.'

— The Haudenoshonee of North America

Every decision we make has an impact; where we spend our money, what corporations or small businesses we support, what food we eat and where we get it from, what policies we allow governments to implement, all of it impacts the next generation.

Have a think about your life, close your eyes and envision the future you want for your descendants. Make a list of ways you are honouring or impeding your vision, and anything you can do to bring about the future you want for them.

September 2026

Notes	Monday	Tuesday	Wednesday
		1	2
	7	8	9
	14	15	16
	21	22	23 *Autumn Equinox*
	28	29	30

Thursday	Friday	Saturday	Sunday
3	4	5	6
10	11	12	13
17	18	19	20
24	25	26	27
1	2	3	4

September
Sappho

SAPPHO

Born sometime around 630 B.C. on the island of Lesbos, Sappho stepped into a world where poetry belonged to men, and she rewrote the rules. Where others sang of war, kings, and conquest, Sappho wrote of the invisible battles of the heart, and was a very talented musician on the Lyre.

Sappho's words were different, she wrote about the heat of longing and the ache of love. In an age obsessed with epic tales of blood and glory, Sappho carved something wild.

Most of her work vanished into history, burned, erased, and dismissed. But yet, the fragments that remain still smoulder. A handful of fragile torn lines that were enough to set the world ablaze.

Sappho gathered around her a circle of women who were poets, musicians and artists. An ancient sanctuary of brilliance and devotion, a place where being female and gifted was sacred.
The centuries tried to silence her. Priests burned her words. Scholars debated her existence. They called her sinful and scandalous. Her name has survived, carried forward by whispers and fragments. Plato called her "the Tenth Muse."
Before the world was ready for her, she was already there.
She was first.
She lit the match.
And she is still burning.

Crystal: Amethyst - to open the emotional channels and find lyrical flow.

My Vision for September

Tuesday | 1 September 2026 - Waning Gibbous

6:00	**Today's quick wins**
7:00	
8:00	
9:00	
10:00	
11:00	**Health and nutrition**
12:00	
13:00	
14:00	**Today, I am grateful for...**
15:00	
16:00	
17:00	**Today's self care**
18:00	
19:00	
20:00	**Chart your cycle**
21:00	
22:00	
23:00	**Positive affirmation**
Notes	

Wednesday | 2 September 2026 - Waning Gibbous

6:00	Today's quick wins	
7:00		
8:00		
9:00		
10:00		
11:00	Health and nutrition	
12:00		
13:00		
14:00	Today, I am grateful for...	
15:00		
16:00		
17:00	Today's self care	
18:00		
19:00		
20:00	Chart your cycle	
21:00		
22:00		
23:00	Positive affirmation	
Notes		

Thursday | 3 September 2026 - Waning Gibbous

6:00		Today's quick wins	
7:00			
8:00			
9:00			
10:00			
11:00		Health and nutrition	
12:00			
13:00			
14:00		Today, I am grateful for...	
15:00			
16:00			
17:00		Today's self care	
18:00			
19:00			
20:00		Chart your cycle	
21:00			
22:00			
23:00		Positive affirmation	
Notes			

Friday | 4 September 2026 - Last Quarter

6:00	Today's quick wins
7:00	
8:00	
9:00	
10:00	
11:00	Health and nutrition
12:00	
13:00	
14:00	Today, I am grateful for...
15:00	
16:00	
17:00	Today's self care
18:00	
19:00	
20:00	Chart your cycle
21:00	
22:00	
23:00	Positive affirmation
Notes	

Saturday | 5 September 2026 - Waning Crescent

6:00	Today's quick wins
7:00	
8:00	
9:00	
10:00	
11:00	Health and nutrition
12:00	
13:00	
14:00	Today, I am grateful for...
15:00	
16:00	
17:00	Today's self care
18:00	
19:00	
20:00	Chart your cycle
21:00	
22:00	
23:00	Positive affirmation
Notes	

Sunday | 6 September 2026 - Waning Crescent

6:00	Today's quick wins	
7:00		
8:00		
9:00		
10:00		
11:00	Health and nutrition	
12:00		
13:00		
14:00	Today, I am grateful for...	
15:00		
16:00		
17:00	Today's self care	
18:00		
19:00		
20:00	Chart your cycle	
21:00		
22:00		
23:00	Positive affirmation	
Notes		

My Week 7th Sep - 13th Sep

Day	
Mon	
Tue	
Wed	
Thu	
Fri	
Sat	
Sun	

Monday | 7 September 2026 - Waning Crescent

6:00	Today's quick wins	
7:00		
8:00		
9:00		
10:00		
11:00	Health and nutrition	
12:00		
13:00		
14:00	Today, I am grateful for…	
15:00		
16:00		
17:00	Today's self care	
18:00		
19:00		
20:00	Chart your cycle	
21:00		
22:00		
23:00	Positive affirmation	
Notes		

Tuesday | 8 September 2026 - Waning Crescent

6:00		Today's quick wins	
7:00			
8:00			
9:00			
10:00			
11:00		Health and nutrition	
12:00			
13:00			
14:00		Today, I am grateful for...	
15:00			
16:00			
17:00		Today's self care	
18:00			
19:00			
20:00		Chart your cycle	
21:00			
22:00			
23:00		Positive affirmation	
Notes			

Wednesday | 9 September 2026 - Waning Crescent

6:00	**Today's quick wins**
7:00	
8:00	
9:00	
10:00	
11:00	**Health and nutrition**
12:00	
13:00	
14:00	**Today, I am grateful for...**
15:00	
16:00	
17:00	**Today's self care**
18:00	
19:00	
20:00	**Chart your cycle**
21:00	
22:00	
23:00	**Positive affirmation**
Notes	

Thursday | 10 September - Waning Crescent

6:00	Today's quick wins	
7:00		
8:00		
9:00		
10:00		
11:00	Health and nutrition	
12:00		
13:00		
14:00	Today, I am grateful for...	
15:00		
16:00		
17:00	Today's self care	
18:00		
19:00		
20:00	Chart your cycle	
21:00		
22:00		
23:00	Positive affirmation	
Notes		

Friday | 11 September 2026 - New Moon in Virgo at 03.26 GMT

6:00	Today's quick wins	
7:00		
8:00		
9:00		
10:00		
11:00	Health and nutrition	
12:00		
13:00		
14:00	Today, I am grateful for...	
15:00		
16:00		
17:00	Today's self care	
18:00		
19:00		
20:00	Chart your cycle	
21:00		
22:00		
23:00	Positive affirmation	
Notes		

Saturday | 12 September 2026 - Waxing Crescent

6:00		Today's quick wins
7:00		
8:00		
9:00		
10:00		
11:00		Health and nutrition
12:00		
13:00		
14:00		Today, I am grateful for...
15:00		
16:00		
17:00		Today's self care
18:00		
19:00		
20:00		Chart your cycle
21:00		
22:00		
23:00		Positive affirmation

Notes

Sunday | 13 September 2026 - Waxing Crescent

6:00	**Today's quick wins**
7:00	
8:00	
9:00	
10:00	
11:00	**Health and nutrition**
12:00	
13:00	
14:00	**Today, I am grateful for...**
15:00	
16:00	
17:00	**Today's self care**
18:00	
19:00	
20:00	**Chart your cycle**
21:00	
22:00	
23:00	**Positive affirmation**
Notes	

My Week 14th Sep - 20th Sep

Mon	
Tue	
Wed	
Thu	
Fri	
Sat	
Sun	

Monday | 14 September 2026 - Waxing Crescent

6:00	Today's quick wins
7:00	
8:00	
9:00	
10:00	
11:00	Health and nutrition
12:00	
13:00	
14:00	Today, I am grateful for...
15:00	
16:00	
17:00	Today's self care
18:00	
19:00	
20:00	Chart your cycle
21:00	
22:00	
23:00	Positive affirmation
Notes	

Tuesday | 15 September 2026 - Waxing Crescent

6:00	**Today's quick wins**
7:00	
8:00	
9:00	
10:00	
11:00	**Health and nutrition**
12:00	
13:00	
14:00	**Today, I am grateful for...**
15:00	
16:00	
17:00	**Today's self care**
18:00	
19:00	
20:00	**Chart your cycle**
21:00	
22:00	
23:00	**Positive affirmation**
Notes	

Wednesday | 16 September 2026 - Waxing Crescent

6:00	**Today's quick wins**
7:00	
8:00	
9:00	
10:00	
11:00	**Health and nutrition**
12:00	
13:00	
14:00	**Today, I am grateful for...**
15:00	
16:00	
17:00	**Today's self care**
18:00	
19:00	
20:00	**Chart your cycle**
21:00	
22:00	
23:00	**Positive affirmation**
Notes	

Thursday | 17 September 2026 - Waxing Crescent

6:00	Today's quick wins
7:00	
8:00	
9:00	
10:00	
11:00	Health and nutrition
12:00	
13:00	
14:00	Today, I am grateful for…
15:00	
16:00	
17:00	Today's self care
18:00	
19:00	
20:00	Chart your cycle
21:00	
22:00	
23:00	Positive affirmation
Notes	

Friday | 18 September 2026 - **First Quarter**

6:00	**Today's quick wins**
7:00	
8:00	
9:00	
10:00	
11:00	**Health and nutrition**
12:00	
13:00	
14:00	**Today, I am grateful for...**
15:00	
16:00	
17:00	**Today's self care**
18:00	
19:00	
20:00	**Chart your cycle**
21:00	
22:00	
23:00	**Positive affirmation**
Notes	

Saturday | 19 September 2026 - First Quarter

6:00	Today's quick wins
7:00	
8:00	
9:00	
10:00	
11:00	Health and nutrition
12:00	
13:00	
14:00	Today, I am grateful for...
15:00	
16:00	
17:00	Today's self care
18:00	
19:00	
20:00	Chart your cycle
21:00	
22:00	
23:00	Positive affirmation
Notes	

Sunday | 20 September 2026 - Waxing Gibbous

6:00	**Today's quick wins**
7:00	
8:00	
9:00	
10:00	
11:00	**Health and nutrition**
12:00	
13:00	
14:00	**Today, I am grateful for...**
15:00	
16:00	
17:00	**Today's self care**
18:00	
19:00	
20:00	**Chart your cycle**
21:00	
22:00	
23:00	**Positive affirmation**
Notes	

My Week 21st Sep - 27th Sep

Mon	
Tue	
Wed	
Thu	
Fri	
Sat	
Sun	

Monday | 21 September 2026 - Waxing Gibbous

6:00	**Today's quick wins**	
7:00		
8:00		
9:00		
10:00		
11:00	**Health and nutrition**	
12:00		
13:00		
14:00	**Today, I am grateful for...**	
15:00		
16:00		
17:00	**Today's self care**	
18:00		
19:00		
20:00	**Chart your cycle**	
21:00		
22:00		
23:00	**Positive affirmation**	
Notes		

Tuesday | 22 September 2026 - Waxing Gibbous

6:00	Today's quick wins	
7:00		
8:00		
9:00		
10:00		
11:00	Health and nutrition	
12:00		
13:00		
14:00	Today, I am grateful for...	
15:00		
16:00		
17:00	Today's self care	
18:00		
19:00		
20:00	Chart your cycle	
21:00		
22:00		
23:00	Positive affirmation	
Notes		

Wednesday | 23 September 2026 - Waxing Gibbous
Autumn Equinox

6:00	Today's quick wins	
7:00		
8:00		
9:00		
10:00		
11:00	Health and nutrition	
12:00		
13:00		
14:00	Today, I am grateful for...	
15:00		
16:00		
17:00	Today's self care	
18:00		
19:00		
20:00	Chart your cycle	
21:00		
22:00		
23:00	Positive affirmation	
Notes		

Thursday | 24 September 2026 - Waxing Gibbous

6:00	Today's quick wins
7:00	
8:00	
9:00	
10:00	
11:00	Health and nutrition
12:00	
13:00	
14:00	Today, I am grateful for...
15:00	
16:00	
17:00	Today's self care
18:00	
19:00	
20:00	Chart your cycle
21:00	
22:00	
23:00	Positive affirmation
Notes	

Friday | 25 September - Waxing Gibbous

6:00	**Today's quick wins**
7:00	
8:00	
9:00	
10:00	
11:00	**Health and nutrition**
12:00	
13:00	
14:00	**Today, I am grateful for...**
15:00	
16:00	
17:00	**Today's self care**
18:00	
19:00	
20:00	**Chart your cycle**
21:00	
22:00	
23:00	**Positive affirmation**
Notes	

Saturday | 26 September 2026 - Full Moon in Aries at 16.48 GMT

6:00	**Today's quick wins**
7:00	
8:00	
9:00	
10:00	
11:00	**Health and nutrition**
12:00	
13:00	
14:00	**Today, I am grateful for...**
15:00	
16:00	
17:00	**Today's self care**
18:00	
19:00	
20:00	**Chart your cycle**
21:00	
22:00	
23:00	**Positive affirmation**
Notes	

Sunday | 27 September 2026 - Waning Gibbous

6:00	Today's quick wins	
7:00		
8:00		
9:00		
10:00		
11:00	Health and nutrition	
12:00		
13:00		
14:00	Today, I am grateful for...	
15:00		
16:00		
17:00	Today's self care	
18:00		
19:00		
20:00	Chart your cycle	
21:00		
22:00		
23:00	Positive affirmation	
Notes		

My Week 28th Sep - 4th Oct

Mon	
Tue	
Wed	
Thu	
Fri	
Sat	
Sun	

Monday | 28 September 2026 - Waning Gibbous

6:00	**Today's quick wins**
7:00	
8:00	
9:00	
10:00	
11:00	**Health and nutrition**
12:00	
13:00	
14:00	**Today, I am grateful for...**
15:00	
16:00	
17:00	**Today's self care**
18:00	
19:00	
20:00	**Chart your cycle**
21:00	
22:00	
23:00	**Positive affirmation**
Notes	

Tuesday | 29 September 2026 - Waning Gibbous

6:00		Today's quick wins	
7:00			
8:00			
9:00			
10:00			
11:00		Health and nutrition	
12:00			
13:00			
14:00		Today, I am grateful for...	
15:00			
16:00			
17:00		Today's self care	
18:00			
19:00			
20:00		Chart your cycle	
21:00			
22:00			
23:00		Positive affirmation	
Notes			

Wednesday | 30 September 2026 - Waning Gibbous

6:00	Today's quick wins
7:00	
8:00	
9:00	
10:00	
11:00	Health and nutrition
12:00	
13:00	
14:00	Today, I am grateful for...
15:00	
16:00	
17:00	Today's self care
18:00	
19:00	
20:00	Chart your cycle
21:00	
22:00	
23:00	Positive affirmation
Notes	

September achievements

Be proud of yourself and all that you have achieved this month. Write down your wins, big and small. If you have not achieved everything that you set out to do, that's okay! We learn and grow through our mistakes and experiences. You can use this space to make notes about anything that you have learned.

"When we are in balance, we are not only healthier, but happier, calmer, and clearer."

— Deepak Chopra

Libra season is the perfect time to pause and reflect on balance.

Where in your life are things flowing with ease, and where might they need more attention?

Make a list of the key areas in your life - for example:

Work or study, Family and relationships, Finances, Fitness and health, Social life, Spiritual or creative life.

Give each area a score from 0 to 10 — 10 meaning you're thriving, 0 meaning you're struggling.

Use these insights as gentle guidance to explore where you can restore harmony and bring your life back into balance.

October 2026

Notes	Monday	Tuesday	Wednesday
	28	29	30
	5	6	7
	12	13	14
	19	20	21
	26	27	28

Thursday	Friday	Saturday	Sunday
1	2	3 ☽	4
8	9	10 ●	11
15	16	17	18 ☾
22	23	24	25
29	30	31	

October
Goddess Durga

DURGA

Durga rides in on a lion looking for war. Eight arms, every one of them holding a weapon.
The gods had been getting their divine backsides handed to them by Mahishasura who was a demon drunk on ego and blood.

Durga was made to end things. She arrives like a storm. No arguing or negotiating, she showed up reminding the universe what divine feminine rage looks like.
She fought for nine nights straight and on the tenth day, she struck the final blow, ending Mahishasura.

Durga shows us that wrath and love aren't opposites. She protects *because* she can destroy.
Durga is the voice inside that says, not today. She's every woman who stood her ground.

She is celebrated during Durga Purja in Sep/Oct every year.
Respected for centuries.
She doesn't just answer prayers, she show's up when we embody her fearlessness in times of need.

Crystal: Black onyx or Hematite to strengthen your protective shield.

My Vision for October

Thursday | 1 October 2026 - Waning Gibbous

6:00	**Today's quick wins**
7:00	
8:00	
9:00	
10:00	
11:00	**Health and nutrition**
12:00	
13:00	
14:00	**Today, I am grateful for…**
15:00	
16:00	
17:00	**Today's self care**
18:00	
19:00	
20:00	**Chart your cycle**
21:00	
22:00	
23:00	**Positive affirmation**
Notes	

Friday | 2 October 2026 - Waning Gibbous

6:00	Today's quick wins
7:00	
8:00	
9:00	
10:00	
11:00	Health and nutrition
12:00	
13:00	
14:00	Today, I am grateful for...
15:00	
16:00	
17:00	Today's self care
18:00	
19:00	
20:00	Chart your cycle
21:00	
22:00	
23:00	Positive affirmation
Notes	

Saturday | 3 October 2026 - Last Quarter

6:00		Today's quick wins
7:00		
8:00		
9:00		
10:00		
11:00		Health and nutrition
12:00		
13:00		
14:00		Today, I am grateful for...
15:00		
16:00		
17:00		Today's self care
18:00		
19:00		
20:00		Chart your cycle
21:00		
22:00		
23:00		Positive affirmation
Notes		

Sunday | 4 October 2026 - Waning Crescent

6:00	**Today's quick wins**
7:00	
8:00	
9:00	
10:00	
11:00	**Health and nutrition**
12:00	
13:00	
14:00	**Today, I am grateful for...**
15:00	
16:00	
17:00	**Today's self care**
18:00	
19:00	
20:00	**Chart your cycle**
21:00	
22:00	
23:00	**Positive affirmation**
Notes	

My Week 5th Oct - 11th Oct

Mon	
Tue	
Wed	
Thu	
Fri	
Sat	
Sun	

Monday | 5 October 2026 - Waning Crescent

6:00	Today's quick wins	
7:00		
8:00		
9:00		
10:00		
11:00	Health and nutrition	
12:00		
13:00		
14:00	Today, I am grateful for...	
15:00		
16:00		
17:00	Today's self care	
18:00		
19:00		
20:00	Chart your cycle	
21:00		
22:00		
23:00	Positive affirmation	
Notes		

Tuesday | 6 October 2026 - Waning Crescent

6:00		Today's quick wins
7:00		
8:00		
9:00		
10:00		
11:00		Health and nutrition
12:00		
13:00		
14:00		Today, I am grateful for...
15:00		
16:00		
17:00		Today's self care
18:00		
19:00		
20:00		Chart your cycle
21:00		
22:00		
23:00		Positive affirmation

Notes

Wednesday | 7 October 2026 - Waning Crescent

6:00	Today's quick wins	
7:00		
8:00		
9:00		
10:00		
11:00	Health and nutrition	
12:00		
13:00		
14:00	Today, I am grateful for...	
15:00		
16:00		
17:00	Today's self care	
18:00		
19:00		
20:00	Chart your cycle	
21:00		
22:00		
23:00	Positive affirmation	
Notes		

Thursday | 8 October 2026 - Waning Crescent

6:00		Today's quick wins
7:00		
8:00		
9:00		
10:00		
11:00		Health and nutrition
12:00		
13:00		
14:00		Today, I am grateful for...
15:00		
16:00		
17:00		Today's self care
18:00		
19:00		
20:00		Chart your cycle
21:00		
22:00		
23:00		Positive affirmation
Notes		

Friday | 9 October 2026 - Waning Crescent

6:00	Today's quick wins
7:00	
8:00	
9:00	
10:00	
11:00	Health and nutrition
12:00	
13:00	
14:00	Today, I am grateful for...
15:00	
16:00	
17:00	Today's self care
18:00	
19:00	
20:00	Chart your cycle
21:00	
22:00	
23:00	Positive affirmation
Notes	

Saturday | 10 October 2026 - New Moon in Libra at 15.49 GMT

6:00	**Today's quick wins**
7:00	
8:00	
9:00	
10:00	
11:00	**Health and nutrition**
12:00	
13:00	
14:00	**Today, I am grateful for...**
15:00	
16:00	
17:00	**Today's self care**
18:00	
19:00	
20:00	**Chart your cycle**
21:00	
22:00	
23:00	**Positive affirmation**
Notes	

Sunday | 11 October 2026 - Waxing Crescent

6:00	**Today's quick wins**
7:00	
8:00	
9:00	
10:00	
11:00	**Health and nutrition**
12:00	
13:00	
14:00	**Today, I am grateful for...**
15:00	
16:00	
17:00	**Today's self care**
18:00	
19:00	
20:00	**Chart your cycle**
21:00	
22:00	
23:00	**Positive affirmation**
Notes	

My Week 12th Oct - 18th Oct

Mon	
Tue	
Wed	
Thu	
Fri	
Sat	
Sun	

Monday | 12 October 2026 - Waxing Crescent

6:00	Today's quick wins	
7:00		
8:00		
9:00		
10:00		
11:00	Health and nutrition	
12:00		
13:00		
14:00	Today, I am grateful for...	
15:00		
16:00		
17:00	Today's self care	
18:00		
19:00		
20:00	Chart your cycle	
21:00		
22:00		
23:00	Positive affirmation	
Notes		

Tuesday | 13 October 2026 - Waxing Crescent

6:00		Today's quick wins
7:00		
8:00		
9:00		
10:00		
11:00		Health and nutrition
12:00		
13:00		
14:00		Today, I am grateful for...
15:00		
16:00		
17:00		Today's self care
18:00		
19:00		
20:00		Chart your cycle
21:00		
22:00		
23:00		Positive affirmation
Notes		

Wednesday | 14 October 2026 - Waxing Crescent

	Today's quick wins
6:00	
7:00	
8:00	
9:00	
10:00	
11:00	Health and nutrition
12:00	
13:00	
14:00	Today, I am grateful for...
15:00	
16:00	
17:00	Today's self care
18:00	
19:00	
20:00	Chart your cycle
21:00	
22:00	
23:00	Positive affirmation
Notes	

Thursday | 15 October 2026 - Waxing Crescent

6:00	**Today's quick wins**
7:00	
8:00	
9:00	
10:00	
11:00	**Health and nutrition**
12:00	
13:00	
14:00	**Today, I am grateful for...**
15:00	
16:00	
17:00	**Today's self care**
18:00	
19:00	
20:00	**Chart your cycle**
21:00	
22:00	
23:00	**Positive affirmation**
Notes	

Friday | 16 October 2026 - Waxing Crescent

6:00		Today's quick wins	
7:00			
8:00			
9:00			
10:00			
11:00		Health and nutrition	
12:00			
13:00			
14:00		Today, I am grateful for...	
15:00			
16:00			
17:00		Today's self care	
18:00			
19:00			
20:00		Chart your cycle	
21:00			
22:00			
23:00		Positive affirmation	
Notes			

Saturday | 17 October 2026 - Waxing Crescent

6:00	**Today's quick wins**
7:00	
8:00	
9:00	
10:00	
11:00	**Health and nutrition**
12:00	
13:00	
14:00	**Today, I am grateful for...**
15:00	
16:00	
17:00	**Today's self care**
18:00	
19:00	
20:00	**Chart your cycle**
21:00	
22:00	
23:00	**Positive affirmation**
Notes	

Sunday | 18 October 2026 - First Quarter

6:00	Today's quick wins	
7:00		
8:00		
9:00		
10:00		
11:00	Health and nutrition	
12:00		
13:00		
14:00	Today, I am grateful for...	
15:00		
16:00		
17:00	Today's self care	
18:00		
19:00		
20:00	Chart your cycle	
21:00		
22:00		
23:00	Positive affirmation	
Notes		

My Week 19th Oct - 25th Oct

Mon	
Tue	
Wed	
Thu	
Fri	
Sat	
Sun	

Monday | 19 October 2026 - Waxing Gibbous

6:00	**Today's quick wins**
7:00	
8:00	
9:00	
10:00	
11:00	**Health and nutrition**
12:00	
13:00	
14:00	**Today, I am grateful for...**
15:00	
16:00	
17:00	**Today's self care**
18:00	
19:00	
20:00	**Chart your cycle**
21:00	
22:00	
23:00	**Positive affirmation**
Notes	

Tuesday | 20 October 2026 - Waxing Gibbous

6:00		Today's quick wins	
7:00			
8:00			
9:00			
10:00			
11:00		Health and nutrition	
12:00			
13:00			
14:00		Today, I am grateful for…	
15:00			
16:00			
17:00		Today's self care	
18:00			
19:00			
20:00		Chart your cycle	
21:00			
22:00			
23:00		Positive affirmation	
Notes			

Wednesday | 21 October 2026 - Waxing Gibbous

6:00	**Today's quick wins**
7:00	
8:00	
9:00	
10:00	
11:00	**Health and nutrition**
12:00	
13:00	
14:00	**Today, I am grateful for...**
15:00	
16:00	
17:00	**Today's self care**
18:00	
19:00	
20:00	**Chart your cycle**
21:00	
22:00	
23:00	**Positive affirmation**
Notes	

Thursday | 22 October 2026 - Waxing Gibbous

6:00	Today's quick wins
7:00	
8:00	
9:00	
10:00	
11:00	Health and nutrition
12:00	
13:00	
14:00	Today, I am grateful for...
15:00	
16:00	
17:00	Today's self care
18:00	
19:00	
20:00	Chart your cycle
21:00	
22:00	
23:00	Positive affirmation
Notes	

Friday | 23 October 2026 - Waxing Gibbous

6:00	Today's quick wins	
7:00		
8:00		
9:00		
10:00		
11:00	Health and nutrition	
12:00		
13:00		
14:00	Today, I am grateful for...	
15:00		
16:00		
17:00	Today's self care	
18:00		
19:00		
20:00	Chart your cycle	
21:00		
22:00		
23:00	Positive affirmation	
Notes		

Saturday | 24 October 2026 - Waxing Gibbous

6:00	**Today's quick wins**
7:00	
8:00	
9:00	
10:00	
11:00	**Health and nutrition**
12:00	
13:00	
14:00	**Today, I am grateful for...**
15:00	
16:00	
17:00	**Today's self care**
18:00	
19:00	
20:00	**Chart your cycle**
21:00	
22:00	
23:00	**Positive affirmation**
Notes	

Sunday | 25 October - Waxing Gibbous

6:00	**Today's quick wins**
7:00	
8:00	
9:00	
10:00	
11:00	**Health and nutrition**
12:00	
13:00	
14:00	**Today, I am grateful for...**
15:00	
16:00	
17:00	**Today's self care**
18:00	
19:00	
20:00	**Chart your cycle**
21:00	
22:00	
23:00	**Positive affirmation**
Notes	

My Week 26th Oct – 1st Nov

Mon	
Tue	
Wed	
Thu	
Fri	
Sat	
Sun	

Monday | 26 October 2026 - Full Moon in Taurus at 04.11 GMT

6:00	**Today's quick wins**
7:00	
8:00	
9:00	
10:00	
11:00	**Health and nutrition**
12:00	
13:00	
14:00	**Today, I am grateful for...**
15:00	
16:00	
17:00	**Today's self care**
18:00	
19:00	
20:00	**Chart your cycle**
21:00	
22:00	
23:00	**Positive affirmation**
Notes	

Tuesday | 27 October 2026 - Waning Gibbous

6:00	**Today's quick wins**
7:00	
8:00	
9:00	
10:00	
11:00	**Health and nutrition**
12:00	
13:00	
14:00	**Today, I am grateful for...**
15:00	
16:00	
17:00	**Today's self care**
18:00	
19:00	
20:00	**Chart your cycle**
21:00	
22:00	
23:00	**Positive affirmation**
Notes	

Wednesday 28 October 2026 - Waning Gibbous

6:00	Today's quick wins	
7:00		
8:00		
9:00		
10:00		
11:00	Health and nutrition	
12:00		
13:00		
14:00	Today, I am grateful for...	
15:00		
16:00		
17:00	Today's self care	
18:00		
19:00		
20:00	Chart your cycle	
21:00		
22:00		
23:00	Positive affirmation	
Notes		

Thursday | 29 October 2026 - Waning Gibbous

6:00		Today's quick wins
7:00		
8:00		
9:00		
10:00		
11:00		Health and nutrition
12:00		
13:00		
14:00		Today, I am grateful for...
15:00		
16:00		
17:00		Today's self care
18:00		
19:00		
20:00		Chart your cycle
21:00		
22:00		
23:00		Positive affirmation
Notes		

Friday | 30 October 2026 - Waning Gibbous

6:00	**Today's quick wins**
7:00	
8:00	
9:00	
10:00	
11:00	**Health and nutrition**
12:00	
13:00	
14:00	**Today, I am grateful for...**
15:00	
16:00	
17:00	**Today's self care**
18:00	
19:00	
20:00	**Chart your cycle**
21:00	
22:00	
23:00	**Positive affirmation**
Notes	

Saturday | 31 October 2026 - Waning Gibbous

6:00	Today's quick wins	
7:00		
8:00		
9:00		
10:00		
11:00	Health and nutrition	
12:00		
13:00		
14:00	Today, I am grateful for...	
15:00		
16:00		
17:00	Today's self care	
18:00		
19:00		
20:00	Chart your cycle	
21:00		
22:00		
23:00	Positive affirmation	
Notes		

October achievements

Be proud of yourself and all that you have achieved this month. Write down your wins, big and small. If you have not achieved everything that you set out to do, that's okay! We learn and grow through our mistakes and experiences. You can use this space to make notes about anything that you have learned.

November 2026

Notes	Monday	Tuesday	Wednesday
	26	27	28
	2	3	4
	9 ●	10	11
	16	17 ◐	18
	23 / 30	24 ○	25

Thursday	Friday	Saturday	Sunday
29	30	31	1
5	6	7	8
12	13	14	15
19	20	21	22
26	27	28	29

November
Goddess Lakshmi

LAKSHMI

Lakshmi's name comes from "Lakṣa", meaning goal, vision, and purpose. She is the guiding light that reminds us that we are worthy, and deserving of abundance. In her presence, prosperity is not limited to gold, it is the inner radiance that blooms fully when we live in harmony with our highest self, our community, and the Earth.

Lakshmi whispers to those who pause long enough to listen: "Abundance is your birthright and generosity is your power."

She invites us to return to our innate wholeness, to remember that true wealth is found not in possessions but in gratitude and compassion.
To honour Lakshmi is to honour the sacred cycles - to receive and to give, to rest and to rise, to bloom and to shed - in rhythm with the currents of life.

She is a gentle current beneath chaos, that shimmering thread of possibility. The Divine Feminine embodied reminding us that when we open ourselves to flow, we become the lotus: rooted, radiant, and infinite.

Crystal: Citrine - holds the warm, golden energy of the sun, dissolving scarcity thinking and connects you to a sense of endless possibility.

My November Vision

"The moon is a loyal companion. It never leaves. It's always there, watching. Steadfast. Knowing us in our light and dark moments."

— Tahereh Mafi

Sunday | 1 November 2026 - Last Quarter

6:00	**Today's quick wins**
7:00	
8:00	
9:00	
10:00	
11:00	**Health and nutrition**
12:00	
13:00	
14:00	**Today, I am grateful for...**
15:00	
16:00	
17:00	**Today's self care**
18:00	
19.00	
20:00	**Chart your cycle**
21:00	
22:00	
23:00	**Positive affirmation**
Notes	

My Week 2nd Nov - 8th Nov

Mon	
Tue	
Wed	
Thu	
Fri	
Sat	
Sun	

Monday | 2 November 2026 - Waning Crescent

6:00	**Today's quick wins**
7:00	
8:00	
9:00	
10:00	
11:00	**Health and nutrition**
12:00	
13:00	
14:00	**Today, I am grateful for...**
15:00	
16:00	
17:00	**Today's self care**
18:00	
19:00	
20:00	**Chart your cycle**
21:00	
22:00	
23:00	**Positive affirmation**
Notes	

Tuesday | 3 November 2026 - Waning Crescent

6:00	**Today's quick wins**
7:00	
8:00	
9:00	
10:00	
11:00	**Health and nutrition**
12:00	
13:00	
14:00	**Today, I am grateful for...**
15:00	
16:00	
17:00	**Today's self care**
18:00	
19:00	
20:00	**Chart your cycle**
21:00	
22:00	
23:00	**Positive affirmation**
Notes	

Wednesday | 4 November 2026 - Waning Crescent

6:00		**Today's quick wins**	
7:00			
8:00			
9:00			
10:00			
11:00		**Health and nutrition**	
12:00			
13:00			
14:00		**Today, I am grateful for...**	
15:00			
16:00			
17:00		**Today's self care**	
18:00			
19:00			
20:00		**Chart your cycle**	
21:00			
22:00			
23:00		**Positive affirmation**	
Notes			

Thursday | 5 November 2026 - Waning Crescent

6:00	Today's quick wins	
7:00		
8:00		
9:00		
10:00		
11:00	Health and nutrition	
12:00		
13:00		
14:00	Today, I am grateful for...	
15:00		
16:00		
17:00	Today's self care	
18:00		
19:00		
20:00	Chart your cycle	
21:00		
22:00		
23:00	Positive affirmation	
Notes		

Friday | 6 November 2026 - Waning Crescent

6:00	Today's quick wins
7:00	
8:00	
9:00	
10:00	
11:00	Health and nutrition
12:00	
13:00	
14:00	Today, I am grateful for...
15:00	
16:00	
17:00	Today's self care
18:00	
19:00	
20:00	Chart your cycle
21:00	
22:00	
23:00	Positive affirmation
Notes	

Saturday | 7 November 2026 - Waning Crescent

6:00	**Today's quick wins**
7:00	
8:00	
9:00	
10:00	
11:00	**Health and nutrition**
12:00	
13:00	
14:00	**Today, I am grateful for...**
15:00	
16:00	
17:00	**Today's self care**
18:00	
19:00	
20:00	**Chart your cycle**
21:00	
22:00	
23:00	**Positive affirmation**
Notes	

Sunday | 8 November - Waning Crescent

6:00	**Today's quick wins**
7:00	
8:00	
9:00	
10:00	
11:00	**Health and nutrition**
12:00	
13:00	
14:00	**Today, I am grateful for...**
15:00	
16:00	
17:00	**Today's self care**
18:00	
19:00	
20:00	**Chart your cycle**
21:00	
22:00	
23:00	**Positive affirmation**
Notes	

My Week 9th Nov - 15th Nov

Mon	
Tue	
Wed	
Thu	
Fri	
Sat	
Sun	

Monday | 9 November 2026 - New Moon in Scorprio at 07.01 GMT

6:00	**Today's quick wins**
7:00	
8:00	
9:00	
10:00	
11:00	**Health and nutrition**
12:00	
13:00	
14:00	**Today, I am grateful for...**
15:00	
16:00	
17:00	**Today's self care**
18:00	
19:00	
20:00	**Chart your cycle**
21:00	
22:00	
23:00	**Positive affirmation**
Notes	

Tuesday | 10 November 2026 - Waxing Crescent

6:00	Today's quick wins
7:00	
8:00	
9:00	
10:00	
11:00	Health and nutrition
12:00	
13:00	
14:00	Today, I am grateful for...
15:00	
16:00	
17:00	Today's self care
18:00	
19:00	
20:00	Chart your cycle
21:00	
22:00	
23:00	Positive affirmation
Notes	

Wednesday | 11 November 2026 - Waxing Crescent

6:00	**Today's quick wins**
7:00	
8:00	
9:00	
10:00	
11:00	**Health and nutrition**
12:00	
13:00	
14:00	**Today, I am grateful for…**
15:00	
16:00	
17:00	**Today's self care**
18:00	
19:00	
20:00	**Chart your cycle**
21:00	
22:00	
23:00	**Positive affirmation**
Notes	

Thursday | 12 November 2026 - Waxing Crescent

6:00	**Today's quick wins**
7:00	
8:00	
9:00	
10:00	
11:00	**Health and nutrition**
12:00	
13:00	
14:00	**Today, I am grateful for...**
15:00	
16:00	
17:00	**Today's self care**
18:00	
19:00	
20:00	**Chart your cycle**
21:00	
22:00	
23:00	**Positive affirmation**
Notes	

Friday | 13 November 2026 - Waxing Crescent

6:00		**Today's quick wins**
7:00		
8:00		
9:00		
10:00		
11:00		**Health and nutrition**
12:00		
13:00		
14:00		**Today, I am grateful for...**
15:00		
16:00		
17:00		**Today's self care**
18:00		
19:00		
20:00		**Chart your cycle**
21:00		
22:00		
23:00		**Positive affirmation**
Notes		

Saturday | 14 November 2026 - Waxing Crescent

6:00	Today's quick wins
7:00	
8:00	
9:00	
10:00	
11:00	Health and nutrition
12:00	
13:00	
14:00	Today, I am grateful for...
15:00	
16:00	
17:00	Today's self care
18:00	
19:00	
20:00	Chart your cycle
21:00	
22:00	
23:00	Positive affirmation
Notes	

Sunday | 15 November 2026 - Waxing Crescent

6:00	**Today's quick wins**
7:00	
8:00	
9:00	
10:00	
11:00	**Health and nutrition**
12:00	
13:00	
14:00	**Today, I am grateful for...**
15:00	
16:00	
17:00	**Today's self care**
18:00	
19:00	
20:00	**Chart your cycle**
21:00	
22:00	
23:00	**Positive affirmation**

Notes

My Week 16th Nov - 22nd Nov

Mon	
Tue	
Wed	
Thu	
Fri	
Sat	
Sun	

Monday | 16 November 2026 - Waxing Crescent

6:00		Today's quick wins
7:00		
8:00		
9:00		
10:00		
11:00		Health and nutrition
12:00		
13:00		
14:00		Today, I am grateful for...
15:00		
16:00		
17:00		Today's self care
18:00		
19:00		
20:00		Chart your cycle
21:00		
22:00		
23:00		Positive affirmation
Notes		

Tuesday | 17 November 2026 - First Quarter

6:00		Today's quick wins
7:00		
8:00		
9:00		
10:00		
11:00		Health and nutrition
12:00		
13:00		
14:00		Today, I am grateful for...
15:00		
16:00		
17:00		Today's self care
18:00		
19:00		
20:00		Chart your cycle
21:00		
22:00		
23:00		Positive affirmation
Notes		

Wednesday | 18 November 2026 - Waxing Gibbous

6:00	Today's quick wins	
7:00		
8:00		
9:00		
10:00		
11:00	Health and nutrition	
12:00		
13:00		
14:00	Today, I am grateful for...	
15:00		
16:00		
17:00	Today's self care	
18:00		
19:00		
20:00	Chart your cycle	
21:00		
22:00		
23:00	Positive affirmation	
Notes		

Thursday | 19 November 2026 - Waxing Gibbous

6:00		Today's quick wins
7:00		
8:00		
9:00		
10:00		
11:00		Health and nutrition
12:00		
13:00		
14:00		Today, I am grateful for...
15:00		
16:00		
17:00		Today's self care
18:00		
19:00		
20:00		Chart your cycle
21:00		
22:00		
23:00		Positive affirmation
Notes		

Friday | 20 November 2026 - Waxing Gibbous

6:00	**Today's quick wins**
7:00	
8:00	
9:00	
10:00	
11:00	**Health and nutrition**
12:00	
13:00	
14:00	**Today, I am grateful for...**
15:00	
16:00	
17:00	**Today's self care**
18:00	
19:00	
20:00	**Chart your cycle**
21:00	
22:00	
23:00	**Positive affirmation**
Notes	

Saturday | 21 November 2026 - Waxing Gibbous

6:00		Today's quick wins
7:00		
8:00		
9:00		
10:00		
11:00		Health and nutrition
12:00		
13:00		
14:00		Today, I am grateful for...
15:00		
16:00		
17:00		Today's self care
18:00		
19:00		
20:00		Chart your cycle
21:00		
22:00		
23:00		Positive affirmation
Notes		

Sunday | 22 November 2026 - Waxing Gibbous

6:00	**Today's quick wins**
7:00	
8:00	
9:00	
10:00	
11:00	**Health and nutrition**
12:00	
13:00	
14:00	**Today, I am grateful for...**
15:00	
16:00	
17:00	**Today's self care**
18:00	
19:00	
20:00	**Chart your cycle**
21:00	
22:00	
23:00	**Positive affirmation**
Notes	

My Week 23rd Nov - 29th Nov

Mon	
Tue	
Wed	
Thu	
Fri	
Sat	
Sun	

Monday | 23 November - Waxing Gibbous

6:00	**Today's quick wins**
7:00	
8:00	
9:00	
10:00	
11:00	**Health and nutrition**
12:00	
13:00	
14:00	**Today, I am grateful for...**
15:00	
16:00	
17:00	**Today's self care**
18:00	
19:00	
20:00	**Chart your cycle**
21:00	
22:00	
23:00	**Positive affirmation**
Notes	

Tuesday | 24 November 2026 - Full Moon in Gemini at 14.53 GMT

6:00	Today's quick wins
7:00	
8:00	
9:00	
10:00	
11:00	Health and nutrition
12:00	
13:00	
14:00	Today, I am grateful for...
15:00	
16:00	
17:00	Today's self care
18:00	
19:00	
20:00	Chart your cycle
21:00	
22:00	
23:00	Positive affirmation
Notes	

Wednesday | 25 November 2026 - Waning Gibbous

6:00	**Today's quick wins**
7:00	
8:00	
9:00	
10:00	
11:00	**Health and nutrition**
12:00	
13:00	
14:00	**Today, I am grateful for...**
15:00	
16:00	
17:00	**Today's self care**
18:00	
19:00	
20:00	**Chart your cycle**
21:00	
22:00	
23:00	**Positive affirmation**
Notes	

Thursday | 26 November 2026 - Waning Gibbous

6:00	**Today's quick wins**
7:00	
8:00	
9:00	
10:00	
11:00	**Health and nutrition**
12:00	
13:00	
14:00	**Today, I am grateful for...**
15:00	
16:00	
17:00	**Today's self care**
18:00	
19:00	
20:00	**Chart your cycle**
21:00	
22:00	
23:00	**Positive affirmation**
Notes	

Friday | 27 November 2026 - Waning Gibbous

6:00	Today's quick wins
7:00	
8:00	
9:00	
10:00	
11:00	Health and nutrition
12:00	
13:00	
14:00	Today, I am grateful for...
15:00	
16:00	
17:00	Today's self care
18:00	
19:00	
20:00	Chart your cycle
21:00	
22:00	
23:00	Positive affirmation
Notes	

Saturday | 28 November 2026 - Waning Gibbous

6:00	**Today's quick wins**
7:00	
8:00	
9:00	
10:00	
11:00	**Health and nutrition**
12:00	
13:00	
14:00	**Today, I am grateful for...**
15:00	
16:00	
17:00	**Today's self care**
18:00	
19:00	
20:00	**Chart your cycle**
21:00	
22:00	
23:00	**Positive affirmation**
Notes	

Sunday | 29 November 2026 - Waning Gibbous

6:00	**Today's quick wins**
7:00	
8:00	
9:00	
10:00	
11:00	**Health and nutrition**
12:00	
13:00	
14:00	**Today, I am grateful for...**
15:00	
16:00	
17:00	**Today's self care**
18:00	
19:00	
20:00	**Chart your cycle**
21:00	
22:00	
23:00	**Positive affirmation**

Notes

My Week 30th Nov – 6th Dec Tue Tue

Mon	
Tue	
Wed	
Thu	
Fri	
Sat	
Sun	

Monday | 30 November 2026 - Waning Gibbous

6:00	Today's quick wins	
7:00		
8:00		
9:00		
10:00		
11:00	Health and nutrition	
12:00		
13:00		
14:00	Today, I am grateful for...	
15:00		
16:00		
17:00	Today's self care	
18:00		
19:00		
20:00	Chart your cycle	
21:00		
22:00		
23:00	Positive affirmation	
Notes		

November achievements

Be proud of yourself and all that you have achieved this month. Write down your wins, big and small. If you have not achieved everything that you set out to do, that's okay! We learn and grow through our mistakes and experiences. You can use this space to make notes about anything that you have learned.

The three most important questions.

1- What do you want to experience in your life?
2- How do you want to grow?
3- What do you want to contribute to the world?

Write your list below. Laying everything out on paper can be really powerful. Feel free to hang this up on a wall somewhere and look at it daily with intention to remind yourself of where you're going. This technique has seen a lot of success and comes from Vishen Lakhiani, founder of Mindvalley.

Experience	Grow	Contribute

December 2026

Notes	Monday	Tuesday	Wednesday
	30	1	2
	7	8	9
	14	15	16
	21 *Winter Solstice*	22	23
	28	29	30

Thursday	Friday	Saturday	Sunday
3	4	5	6
10	11	12	13
17	18	19	20
24	25	26	27
31	1	2	3

December
Goddess Circe

CIRCE

Daughter of Helios, blood of Titans, she forged her own name in potion and patience. The gods called her soft and too strange. Men called her dangerous - and they were right, she turned some of them into swine.

Circe isn't just myth, she's the blueprint for every woman who's ever been too powerful to control. She's the high priestess: not quite mortal, not quite divine.
Cast out by her own kin which is when her magic woke up.

Her island, Aiaia is more of a portal than a paradise. A place between worlds where any visitor would find the grimoire open.

Her magic is a craft, learned and embodied, she knows every name of the plants that heal and poison. Her exile was an initiation and her solitude became her awakening.

Circe is every woman who's ever been underestimated and answered with alchemy.

Gather your herbs and let the cauldron bubble.

Crystal: Labradorite - the sorceress's stone, it strengthens psychic vision, dreamwork, and hidden knowledge. Perfect for channeling Circe's gift of transformation and unseen power.

My Vision for December

Tuesday | 1 December 2026 - Last Quarter

6:00		Today's quick wins
7:00		
8:00		
9:00		
10:00		
11:00		Health and nutrition
12:00		
13:00		
14:00		Today, I am grateful for...
15:00		
16:00		
17:00		Today's self care
18:00		
19:00		
20:00		Chart your cycle
21:00		
22:00		
23:00		Positive affirmation
Notes		

Wednesday | 2 December 2026 - Waning Crescent

6:00	**Today's quick wins**
7:00	
8:00	
9:00	
10:00	
11:00	**Health and nutrition**
12:00	
13:00	
14:00	**Today, I am grateful for...**
15:00	
16:00	
17:00	**Today's self care**
18:00	
19:00	
20:00	**Chart your cycle**
21:00	
22:00	
23:00	**Positive affirmation**
Notes	

Thursday | 3 December 2026 - Waning Crescent

6:00	Today's quick wins	
7:00		
8:00		
9:00		
10:00		
11:00	Health and nutrition	
12:00		
13:00		
14:00	Today, I am grateful for…	
15:00		
16:00		
17:00	Today's self care	
18:00		
19:00		
20:00	Chart your cycle	
21:00		
22:00		
23:00	Positive affirmation	
Notes		

Friday | 4 December 2026 - Waning Crescent

6:00		Today's quick wins
7:00		
8:00		
9:00		
10:00		
11:00		Health and nutrition
12:00		
13:00		
14:00		Today, I am grateful for…
15:00		
16:00		
17:00		Today's self care
18:00		
19:00		
20:00		Chart your cycle
21:00		
22:00		
23:00		Positive affirmation
Notes		

Saturday | 5 December 2026 - Waning Crescent

6:00	Today's quick wins
7:00	
8:00	
9:00	
10:00	
11:00	Health and nutrition
12:00	
13:00	
14:00	Today, I am grateful for...
15:00	
16:00	
17:00	Today's self care
18:00	
19:00	
20:00	Chart your cycle
21:00	
22:00	
23:00	Positive affirmation
Notes	

Sunday | 6 December 2026 - Waning Crescent

6:00	**Today's quick wins**
7:00	
8:00	
9:00	
10:00	
11:00	**Health and nutrition**
12:00	
13:00	
14:00	**Today, I am grateful for...**
15:00	
16:00	
17:00	**Today's self care**
18:00	
19:00	
20:00	**Chart your cycle**
21:00	
22:00	
23:00	**Positive affirmation**
Notes	

My Week 7th Dec - 14th Dec

Mon	
Tue	
Wed	
Thu	
Fri	
Sat	
Sun	

Monday | 7 December 2026 - Waning Crescent

6:00	**Today's quick wins**
7:00	
8:00	
9:00	
10:00	
11:00	**Health and nutrition**
12:00	
13:00	
14:00	**Today, I am grateful for...**
15:00	
16:00	
17:00	**Today's self care**
18:00	
19:00	
20:00	**Chart your cycle**
21:00	
22:00	
23:00	**Positive affirmation**
Notes	

Tuesday | 8 December - Waning Crescent

6:00	**Today's quick wins**
7:00	
8:00	
9:00	
10:00	
11:00	**Health and nutrition**
12:00	
13:00	
14:00	**Today, I am grateful for...**
15:00	
16:00	
17:00	**Today's self care**
18:00	
19:00	
20:00	**Chart your cycle**
21:00	
22:00	
23:00	**Positive affirmation**

Notes

Wednesday | 9 December 2026 - New Moon in Sagittarius at 00.51 GMT

6:00	Today's quick wins
7:00	
8:00	
9:00	
10:00	
11:00	Health and nutrition
12:00	
13:00	
14:00	Today, I am grateful for...
15:00	
16:00	
17:00	Today's self care
18:00	
19.00	
20:00	Chart your cycle
21:00	
22:00	
23:00	Positive affirmation
Notes	

Thursday | 10 December 2026 - Waxing Crescent

6:00		Today's quick wins
7:00		
8:00		
9:00		
10:00		
11:00		Health and nutrition
12:00		
13:00		
14:00		Today, I am grateful for...
15:00		
16:00		
17:00		Today's self care
18:00		
19:00		
20:00		Chart your cycle
21:00		
22:00		
23:00		Positive affirmation
Notes		

Friday | 11 December 2026 - Waxing Crescent

6:00	**Today's quick wins**
7:00	
8:00	
9:00	
10:00	
11:00	**Health and nutrition**
12:00	
13:00	
14:00	**Today, I am grateful for...**
15:00	
16:00	
17:00	**Today's self care**
18:00	
19:00	
20:00	**Chart your cycle**
21:00	
22:00	
23:00	**Positive affirmation**

Notes

Saturday | 12 December 2026 - Waxing Crescent

6:00	Today's quick wins
7:00	
8:00	
9:00	
10:00	
11:00	Health and nutrition
12:00	
13:00	
14:00	Today, I am grateful for...
15:00	
16:00	
17:00	Today's self care
18:00	
19:00	
20:00	Chart your cycle
21:00	
22:00	
23:00	Positive affirmation
Notes	

Sunday | 13 December 2026 - Waxing Crescent

6:00	**Today's quick wins**
7:00	
8:00	
9:00	
10:00	
11:00	**Health and nutrition**
12:00	
13:00	
14:00	**Today, I am grateful for...**
15:00	
16:00	
17:00	**Today's self care**
18:00	
19:00	
20:00	**Chart your cycle**
21:00	
22:00	
23:00	**Positive affirmation**
Notes	

My Week 14th Dec - 20th Dec

Mon	
Tue	
Wed	
Thu	
Fri	
Sat	
Sun	

Monday | 14 December 2026 - Waxing Crescent

6:00	**Today's quick wins**
7:00	
8:00	
9:00	
10:00	
11:00	**Health and nutrition**
12:00	
13:00	
14:00	**Today, I am grateful for...**
15:00	
16:00	
17:00	**Today's self care**
18:00	
19:00	
20:00	**Chart your cycle**
21:00	
22:00	
23:00	**Positive affirmation**
Notes	

Tuesday | 15 December 2026 - Waxing Crescent

6:00		Today's quick wins
7:00		
8:00		
9:00		
10:00		
11:00		Health and nutrition
12:00		
13:00		
14:00		Today, I am grateful for...
15:00		
16:00		
17:00		Today's self care
18:00		
19:00		
20:00		Chart your cycle
21:00		
22:00		
23:00		Positive affirmation
Notes		

Wednesday | 16 December 2026 - Waxing Crescent

6:00	Today's quick wins	
7:00		
8:00		
9:00		
10:00		
11:00	Health and nutrition	
12:00		
13:00		
14:00	Today, I am grateful for…	
15:00		
16:00		
17:00	Today's self care	
18:00		
19:00		
20:00	Chart your cycle	
21:00		
22:00		
23:00	Positive affirmation	
Notes		

Thursday | 17 December 2026 - First Quarter

6:00		Today's quick wins
7:00		
8:00		
9:00		
10:00		
11:00		Health and nutrition
12:00		
13:00		
14:00		Today, I am grateful for...
15:00		
16:00		
17:00		Today's self care
18:00		
19:00		
20:00		Chart your cycle
21:00		
22:00		
23:00		Positive affirmation
Notes		

Friday | 18 December 2026 - Waxing Gibbous

6:00	**Today's quick wins**
7:00	
8:00	
9:00	
10:00	
11:00	**Health and nutrition**
12:00	
13:00	
14:00	**Today, I am grateful for...**
15:00	
16:00	
17:00	**Today's self care**
18:00	
19:00	
20:00	**Chart your cycle**
21:00	
22:00	
23:00	**Positive affirmation**
Notes	

Saturday | 19 December 2026 - Waxing Gibbous

6:00	**Today's quick wins**
7:00	
8:00	
9:00	
10:00	
11:00	**Health and nutrition**
12:00	
13:00	
14:00	**Today, I am grateful for...**
15:00	
16:00	
17:00	**Today's self care**
18:00	
19:00	
20:00	**Chart your cycle**
21:00	
22:00	
23:00	**Positive affirmation**

Notes

Sunday | 20 December 2026 - Waxing Gibbous

6:00	**Today's quick wins**
7:00	
8:00	
9:00	
10:00	
11:00	**Health and nutrition**
12:00	
13:00	
14:00	**Today, I am grateful for...**
15:00	
16:00	
17:00	**Today's self care**
18:00	
19:00	
20:00	**Chart your cycle**
21:00	
22:00	
23:00	**Positive affirmation**
Notes	

My Week 21st Dec - 27th Dec

Mon	
Tue	
Wed	
Thu	
Fri	
Sat	
Sun	

Monday | 21 December 2026 - Waxing Gibbous
Winter Solstice

6:00		Today's quick wins
7:00		
8:00		
9:00		
10:00		
11:00		Health and nutrition
12:00		
13:00		
14:00		Today, I am grateful for...
15:00		
16:00		
17:00		Today's self care
18:00		
19:00		
20:00		Chart your cycle
21:00		
22:00		
23:00		Positive affirmation
Notes		

Tuesday | 22 December 2026 - Waxing Gibbous

6:00	**Today's quick wins**
7:00	
8:00	
9:00	
10:00	
11:00	**Health and nutrition**
12:00	
13:00	
14:00	**Today, I am grateful for...**
15:00	
16:00	
17:00	**Today's self care**
18:00	
19:00	
20:00	**Chart your cycle**
21:00	
22:00	
23:00	**Positive affirmation**
Notes	

Wednesday 23 December - Waxing Gibbous

6:00	Today's quick wins
7:00	
8:00	
9:00	
10:00	
11:00	Health and nutrition
12:00	
13:00	
14:00	Today, I am grateful for...
15:00	
16:00	
17:00	Today's self care
18:00	
19:00	
20:00	Chart your cycle
21:00	
22:00	
23:00	Positive affirmation
Notes	

Thursday | 24 December 2026 - Full Moon in Cancer at 01.27 GMT

6:00	Today's quick wins
7:00	
8:00	
9:00	
10:00	
11:00	Health and nutrition
12:00	
13:00	
14:00	Today, I am grateful for...
15:00	
16:00	
17:00	Today's self care
18:00	
19:00	
20:00	Chart your cycle
21:00	
22:00	
23:00	Positive affirmation
Notes	

Friday | 25 December 2026 - Waning Gibbous

6:00		Today's quick wins	
7:00			
8:00			
9:00			
10:00			
11:00		Health and nutrition	
12:00			
13:00			
14:00		Today, I am grateful for...	
15:00			
16:00			
17:00		Today's self care	
18:00			
19:00			
20:00		Chart your cycle	
21:00			
22:00			
23:00		Positive affirmation	
Notes			

Saturday | 26 December 2026 - Waning Gibbous

6:00	**Today's quick wins**
7:00	
8:00	
9:00	
10:00	
11:00	**Health and nutrition**
12:00	
13:00	
14:00	**Today, I am grateful for...**
15:00	
16:00	
17:00	**Today's self care**
18:00	
19:00	
20:00	**Chart your cycle**
21:00	
22:00	
23:00	**Positive affirmation**
Notes	

Sunday | 27 December 2026 - Waning Gibbous

6:00		**Today's quick wins**
7:00		
8:00		
9:00		
10:00		
11:00		**Health and nutrition**
12:00		
13:00		
14:00		**Today, I am grateful for...**
15:00		
16:00		
17:00		**Today's self care**
18:00		
19:00		
20:00		**Chart your cycle**
21:00		
22:00		
23:00		**Positive affirmation**

Notes

My Week 28th Dec – 3rd Jan

Mon	
Tue	
Wed	
Thu	
Fri	
Sat	
Sun	

Monday | 28 December 2026 - Waning Gibbous

6:00	Today's quick wins
7:00	
8:00	
9:00	
10:00	
11:00	Health and nutrition
12:00	
13:00	
14:00	Today, I am grateful for...
15:00	
16:00	
17:00	Today's self care
18:00	
19:00	
20:00	Chart your cycle
21:00	
22:00	
23:00	Positive affirmation
Notes	

Tuesday | 29 December 2026 - Waning Gibbous

6:00	Today's quick wins	
7:00		
8:00		
9:00		
10:00		
11:00	Health and nutrition	
12:00		
13:00		
14:00	Today, I am grateful for...	
15:00		
16:00		
17:00	Today's self care	
18:00		
19:00		
20:00	Chart your cycle	
21:00		
22:00		
23:00	Positive affirmation	
Notes		

Wednesday | 30 December 2026 - Last Quarter

6:00	Today's quick wins	
7:00		
8:00		
9:00		
10:00		
11:00	Health and nutrition	
12:00		
13:00		
14:00	Today, I am grateful for...	
15:00		
16:00		
17:00	Today's self care	
18:00		
19:00		
20:00	Chart your cycle	
21:00		
22:00		
23:00	Positive affirmation	
Notes		

Thursday | 31 December 2026 - Waning Crescent

6:00	Today's quick wins	
7:00		
8:00		
9:00		
10:00		
11:00	Health and nutrition	
12:00		
13:00		
14:00	Today, I am grateful for...	
15:00		
16:00		
17:00	Today's self care	
18:00		
19:00		
20:00	Chart your cycle	
21:00		
22:00		
23:00	Positive affirmation	
Notes		

December achievements

Be proud of yourself and all that you have achieved this month. Write down your wins, big and small. If you have not achieved everything that you set out to do, that's okay! We learn and grow through our mistakes and experiences. You can use this space to make notes about anything that you have learned.

What have I achieved and how have I grown in 2026...

My 2026 Reading List.

Film & Podcast Notes

Notes

Notes

Notes

Vision for 2027

www.ingramcontent.com/pod-product-compliance
Lightning Source LLC
Chambersburg PA
CBHW070043230426
43661CB00005B/736